# THE GUIDE

# Colorado
# Birds

## MARY TAYLOR GRAY

PHOTOGRAPHY BY HERBERT CLARKE

WESTCLIFFE PUBLISHERS

# CONTENTS

2/99

**COLOR TAB INDEX TO BIRD CATEGORIES**

ISBN: 1-56579-283-1

**Designer:** Paulette Livers Lambert
**Production Manager:** Harlene Finn
**Editor:** Betty Taylor
**Technical Editor:** Mike Carter, the Colorado Bird Observatory

Published by
WESTCLIFFE PUBLISHERS, INC.
P. O. Box 1261
Englewood, Colorado 80150

Printed in Hong Kong through World Print Ltd.

Library of Congress Cataloging-in-Publication Data
Gray, Mary Taylor, 1955–
        The guide to Colorado birds / by Mary Taylor Gray ; photography by
    Herbert Clarke ; foreword by Michael F. Carter.
            p.  cm.
    Includes bibliographical references and index.
    ISBN 1-56579-283-1
        1. Birds—Colorado.        I. Title.
    QL684.C6C735   1998
    598'.09788—dc21                                                98-9635
                                                                    CIP

*For more information about other fine books and calendars from
Westcliffe Publishers, please call your local bookstore, contact us at
1-800-523-3692, or write for our free color catalog.*

**Cover photos: Left to right, top row:** *Western Tanager, Bald Eagle,
Mountain Bluebird;* **middle row:** *Great Horned Owl, Wood Duck,
Broad-tailed Hummingbird;* **bottom row:** *Steller's Jay, Golden Eagle,
Yellow-headed Blackbird.*
**Opposite:** *American Goldfinch*

## Contents

# FOREWORD

I often try to relate to others the wealth of ornithological resources with which Colorado is blessed, and, as a biologist, I resort to facts and figures. Thank goodness there are writers like Mary Taylor Gray who are able to relate their experiences with words. From a biologist's perspective, there are 277 species of birds that nest within the borders of our state. Theoretically, a person with lots of spare time and knowledge could see all 277 species during the month of June. This June breeding bird total in Colorado is exceeded only by a handful of other states. During the rest of the year, our active bird-watcher could possibly see another 90 species. And during a lifetime of birding in Colorado, another 50 could be added to bring the "life list" total to more than 400.

Of course, these are high numbers, only accumulated by someone devoting every spare moment to finding a "needed" species. My point is not so much about the process of listing birds (a common pursuit among bird-watchers), but about the fact that Colorado is a rich hunting ground for bird-watchers. Beginning bird-watchers could easily see more than 200 species of birds within Colorado in one year. They could also see 30–40 species in their backyards every year, 60 on a day-long field trip, a few hundred on a bird-watching vacation, and possibly more than a thousand in a lifetime of bird-watching with a spouse.

I challenge you to name a hundred of anything with which you are familiar. I guess some of us might have collections of coins, stamps, and other collectibles that number in the hundreds or thousands. "Collecting" birds that frequent our lives provides the foundation for bird-watching. Each species, by definition, is different and you end up wanting to see more and more. They build different nests in different locations; some spend the winter in far-flung places; others use beautiful plumage or displays to attract mates; they use different habitats, or are found in every habitat. If you spend a year looking at birds, you will be collecting sightings of species, but you will also note hundreds of songs, plumages, behaviors, and habitats. All of these factors (plus the fact that people just like to be outdoors) contribute to the popularity that the sport of birdwatching is currently enjoying. It has become so popular that it has a new name—birding. Part of this interest has been driven by better information available about birds, and this book by Mary Taylor Gray certainly falls in that category.

What causes such a diversity of birds in Colorado? Undoubtedly, the variety of habitats drives the high diversity of birds found within our state. We have alpine tundra, aspen forests, cotton-wood woodlands, piñon-pine woodlands, and prairie grasslands. Each habitat has its own community of birds with each species having its own story. Although Colorado is known for its mountains, my favorite birding is on the plains. Within Colorado there are even different kinds of prairies, each hosting its own community of birds. For instance, sand sage prairie is the home of Upland Sandpipers, Greater Prairie-Chickens, and Grasshopper Sparrows; and the shortgrass prairie is home to Mountain Plovers, McCown's Longspurs, and our state bird, the Lark Bunting.

The Lark Bunting often gets a bum rap for being just a black and white bird. It has been said that it was chosen as our state bird because it would only require black ink to print (no color!). But what the Lark Bunting lacks in color, it more than makes up for in behavior. Make one visit to a shortgrass prairie in May to be accosted by skylarking displays of Lark Buntings, and you'll understand why it was really chosen. Additionally, maybe it was chosen because it was once found in the millions on Colorado's prairies. They were so abundant that early settlers often commented in their letters and journals about the millions of black and white birds. I'm sure millions of skylarking Lark Buntings made a lasting impression on them.

The Lark Bunting's fate was once tied to bison, prairie, weather, and eons of time. Now their fate (and that of many other bird species) is tied to landowners and conservation organizations who care, agencies trying to balance increasing needs forced upon the land, and those who are just trying to get them into the next century. Because Lark Buntings are migratory, they depend on the goodwill of two countries, the U.S. and Mexico. And because people have become so abundant, they are dependent upon us to do the right thing.

I urge you as you are bitten by the birding bug (and even if you're not) to give something back to birds. Improve the habitat in your backyard; be active to improve or restore native habitats; or assist with purchasing pristine lands for birds. As you develop expertise, help with bird monitoring, research, or education projects—there are many possibilities. Of course, one of the best organizations for the birds is the one for which I work. Consider becoming a member!

Finally, enjoy the birds. I hope this guide is helpful in your endeavor.

Michael Carter
Colorado Bird Observatory

*To my daughter Olivia, who was incubating
at the same time as this book*

# ACKNOWLEDGMENTS

From initial courtship to fledging, this book took flight with the help of many people. I'd like to thank Scott Menough, owner of two Wild Birds Unlimited stores in the Denver area, for his input on the initial species list; Mike Carter, Director of the Colorado Bird Observatory, for his extensive work reviewing and checking the manuscript and for writing the foreword; Bob Hernbrode, Watchable Wildlife Coordinator for the Colorado Division of Wildlife, for his review and suggestions on the Colorado Birding Tips; Jerry Craig, Division of Wildlife raptor biologist, for helping with status and population information on falcons, eagles, and mountain plovers; my husband, Rick Young, for his support and patience as I toiled on this book; and finally, John Fielder and all the staff at Westcliffe Publishers for understanding that Colorado's priceless outdoor heritage includes far more than just scenery and for wanting to produce a user-friendly bird guide to help both Coloradans and visitors more fully appreciate the wildlife wonders of our exceptional state.

# INTRODUCTION

Colorado boasts a wonderful variety of colorful and interesting birds that are an important part of our state's outdoor heritage. Birds enliven our prairies and mountains, canyons and forests, bringing an added component of color, sound, and vitality to Colorado's scenic beauties.

Bird-watching, or birding, is no longer an esoteric hobby of stuffy eccentrics wearing pith helmets and sturdy shoes. Anyone can watch birds; in fact, some 70 million Americans do. Today birding ranks behind only gardening as the most popular hobby in America. The reasons are many. Watching birds gets you outdoors, connects you to nature, sharpens your senses and observation skills, brings you in contact with others of similar interests, introduces an entire new base of knowledge, and is lots of fun! It requires little equipment and as little or as much time, energy, and exertion as you wish to invest. Birding is a hobby for everyone and can be enjoyed in your backyard or in exotic places far from home. Some watchers become passionate and acquire vast knowledge about birds. Others enjoy birding only occasionally or as an adjunct to other outdoor recreation. Whatever your style, remember that birding is not a competition. What matters is not how many birds you see but that you take pleasure from seeing them.

Whether you are visiting our state on summer vacation and want to know a little more about the birds you see, or are a Coloradan seeking to broaden your appreciation of your home's natural treasures, I hope *The Guide to Colorado Birds* is a useful and enjoyable resource.

***Hermit Thrush***

# HOW TO USE THIS GUIDE

There are a great many bird guides on the market, from excellent standards such as the *National Geographic Field Guide to the Birds of North America* to regional guides detailing bird species likely to be seen in an area. But these general guides often do not serve the needs of local birders because they encompass too broad an area and too many species while lacking local information. *The Guide to Colorado Birds* fills the need for a state-specific guide, with current and accurate information about when and where to view birds in this state. This book does not include every single species ever seen in Colorado, but instead offers a strong selection of birds found here at various times of the year and that watchers have a good chance of seeing.

## Organization of Species

Species are grouped into 21 categories of related or physically similar birds. The sequence generally follows the American Ornithologists' Union (AOU) checklist for taxonomic order, though some birds are grouped out of order to facilitate identification. For example, swallows are grouped with swifts, and the House Sparrow with other sparrows. In addition

*Migrating Shorebirds*

*Franklin's Gulls*

a few lone species, such as the Belted Kingfisher, are grouped in
with a different family. The Colorado species covered in this
book are listed in accurate taxonomic order at the back of the
book, according to the current AOU checklist.

## Species Profiles

Two hundred thirty-six species of Colorado birds are
profiled. Twenty-three additional less common species are
mentioned in bold type within the profile of a similar or
related bird. For example, the Bohemian Waxwing is mentioned within the Field Notes section of the Cedar Waxwing
profile. Three sets of "clustered profiles"—on sandpipers,
empidonax flycatchers, and sparrows—cover, in abbreviated
form, groups of birds that are either in Colorado for only
short periods or are all quite similar and therefore very difficult
for the casual birder to identify. The clusters present a para-
graph of text and a photograph of each of these species for
easy comparison.

## Anatomy of a Species Profile

**Common Name** is the accepted common name for the bird, followed by its **Scientific Name,** based upon the 41st supplement to the AOU checklist, issued in 1997. This explains why some readers will encounter new and unfamiliar species— Juniper Titmouse and Plumbeous Vireo—while missing more familiar names that have now been replaced, such as Plain Titmouse and Solitary Vireo.

**Field ID** provides a brief physical description of the bird, including male versus female and seasonal plumages when applicable. Where there is no great difference, only one description is given. **Size** is the average length, in inches, of study skins of this species. Study skins are measured from tip of beak to tip of tail with the skin laid on its back and the beak extended straight up. These figures are taken from the *National Geographic Field Guide to the Birds of North America.* Where there is great variation in size, a range is given.

**Habitat** describes the general habitats or natural communities in which each species is found, with the preferred habitat listed first.

*Hummingbirds at feeder*

**Field Notes** present a distinctive aspect of the species' behavior or natural history, and when and where it is generally found in the state.

**Color Tabbed Pages** allow readers to flip quickly to groups of birds. Tabs correspond to the Color Tab Index on page one. Each species' particular family is noted within the color tab. The Quick Reference Index to Species and Families inside the front cover is another easy-reference guide.

**Calendar Bar** graphic shows the months of the year when the species can be seen in Colorado. Months shown in palest blue represent times when the bird is not present in Colorado. Months shown in medium blue represent times when the bird is present in moderate numbers. Months shown in dark blue represent times when the bird is present in moderate to abundant numbers. The calendar bar applies to the main bird profiled, not to secondary species mentioned in bold type. Pages with clusters do not have calendar bars, but each species' seasonality in Colorado is mentioned in the text.

**Jan Feb Mar** Apr May June July Aug Sept Oct **Nov Dec**

**Mary Taylor Gray's Colorado Birding Tips** are 40 vignettes scattered throughout the book that offer Colorado-specific tips for viewing birds in our state, or highlight particular behaviors to watch and listen for when birding in Colorado. Detailed descriptions or directions to sites are limited by space. For very specific information and directions for viewing individual species, see *The Birders Guide to Colorado* by Harold Holt. For an overview of "110 Watchable Wildlife" viewing areas in the state, see the *Colorado Wildlife Viewing Guide* by Mary Taylor Gray. For help in locating sites mentioned in the text, see the *Colorado Atlas and Gazetteer*.

**Photographs** identifying adult birds are presented for each species. When male and female are not significantly different in appearance, only one photo is offered. When male and female are different, both are shown. Birds are generally shown in breeding plumage, except when the species is mainly seen in Colorado in winter plumage. With a few exceptions, immature birds and multiple age classes are not represented.

*15*

# BIRDING BASICS

## *Optics*

Binoculars are probably the single most helpful tool in the birder's repertoire. The nuances of binocular selection are complicated, so learn all you can from your retailer, then buy the best you can afford. Binoculars are labeled with a pair of numbers such as 7x35 or 8x40. The first number is the magnification (7x = seven times). While 7x binoculars don't magnify images as large as 10x, lower powered binoculars generally focus closer than higher powered ones, making it easier to see birds close to you.

The second number, the diameter of the objective lens, represents the amount of light entering the binoculars. The larger the number, the more light, so the better the viewing in low-light conditions such as dawn or dusk.

New birders should wait to invest in a spotting scope. Scopes are wonderful tools for birding but expensive and cumbersome and generally not a good idea for beginners.

*Birders in the field*

## In the Field

Plan to venture out at the times of day when birds are most active—morning and evening. Head for places that offer good bird habitat—waterways, undeveloped land, edges of farm fields, woodlands. Wear clothing of muted colors like brown or gray so that you are less obvious; birds see color well and a white shirt will make you stand out like a flag. Wear layers so that you can adjust to changing weather—a cold Colorado morning soon turns hot when the sun gets well up. Protect your eyes with good sunglasses and your skin with sunblock. A hat is also a good idea.

## How to Watch

Move quietly and slowly, watching for sound and movement. When you find a promising area that seems to have a lot of bird activity, find a comfortable spot and settle down. Once you are still, the birds will reemerge. When you spot a bird, keep your eyes on it and lift your binoculars into your line of vision.

Don't burden yourself with trying to instantly identify every bird. Instead, note the following:

**Size**—Compared with familiar birds, is it the size of a sparrow, a robin, a crow?

**Shape and Body Parts**—Is it long and slender, round and plump, standing on long legs? Is its tail especially long or its beak heavy and thick?

**Posture**—Does it perch particularly upright, is it bent over, or does it cling to the side of a tree?

**Color, patterns, stripes, or other field marks**—Is it mottled or striped, painted in blocks of color? Does it have a bold eye ring, a dark cap, or bars on the wings?

**Behavior**—What is the bird doing? Is it swooping out and back from a perch, foraging for insects in the grass, wading in shallow water?

**Habitat**—Make note of your surroundings. Are you in a pine forest, at the edge of a cattail wetland, in a sagebrush upland?

Some birds are easy to identify at a glance, while others will require adding up everything you've noticed, including habitat, then making an educated guess.

# COLORADO'S ECOSYSTEMS

From the southeastern edge of the state at an elevation of 3,350 feet to the top of our highest peak, Mount Elbert, at 14,433 feet, Colorado is a state of diverse natural communities. Differing conditions of moisture, weather, and topography on the Eastern versus Western Slopes also affect the resulting plant communities. While some birds are tied closely to particular ecosystems or habitats, many birds make use of more than one habitat during the year. Songbirds nesting in a montane forest, for example, may move into the subalpine forest after their young have left the nest in order to take advantage of the rich, late summer resources of this moist habitat. Many species are found broadly distributed across Colorado's ecosystems during migration.

Recent study of Colorado's natural communities by biologists at the Denver Museum of Natural History resulted in the definition of eight ecosystems within Colorado. Within each of these ecosystems are a variety of specific habitats.

**Grassland**—Found in the eastern half of the state, this semiarid environment, receiving an average of 15 inches of precipitation annually, is dominated by short grasses, shrubs, and forbs (flowering, nonwoody plants). Trees typically grow only along waterways. Today perhaps only 10 percent of native prairie remains, most having been converted to cultivated farm fields and grazing pasture.

**Riparian**—Literally meaning "near water," riparian habitats are moist areas found along streams, rivers, ponds, and other water sources, from the plains to the alpine tundra. They include cattail marshes, wetlands, streamside cottonwood groves, willow thickets, wet meadows, and much more. Nearly 75 percent of wildlife depend to some degree upon riparian habitats.

**Montane Shrublands**—This is a transition zone from the prairies to the mountains. In some ways synonymous with the foothills life zone, it is mainly found on the Eastern Slope. This community is dominated by shrubs such as mountain mahogany and Gambel oak, with some incursion of ponderosa pine and Douglas-fir.

**Montane Forests**—Above the foothills shrublands lie the forests of the montane zone. Here ponderosa pine dominate on hot, dry, south-facing slopes, and Douglas-fir prevail on moist, cool, north-facing slopes. Stands of aspen and lodgepole pine move into areas of fire, avalanche, or other disturbance.

**Semidesert Shrublands**—Different conditions on the Western Slope versus the Eastern Slope dictate different plant communities. In contrast to eastern grasslands, the semidesert shrublands of western Colorado are typically dry, rough, broken country dominated by big sagebrush as well as greasewood, four-winged saltbush, rabbitbrush, and other shrubs.

**Piñon Pine/Juniper Woodlands**—This open, rolling, semi-arid country found across southern Colorado might not look like a woodland to many, though the stands of piñon pine and juniper, the dominant trees, can be quite extensive. Interspersed are open, dry meadows of grasses, cactus, shrubs, and forbs.

**Subalpine Forest**—These thick, moist, high-altitude forests are dominated by subalpine fir and Engelmann spruce, extending from the montane forests to timberline. Stunted, wind-sculpted timber stands known as krummholz mark the treeline.

**Alpine Tundra**—This treeless land at the very top of Colorado is home to low-growing forbs, ground-hugging shrubs, grasses, and willow thickets around moist pockets. It is punctuated by boulder fields, rock gardens, and talus slopes.

# ETHICS AND ETIQUETTE

When watching birds, remember that you are in essence entering the animals' "home" and should conduct yourself as a guest. Respect the birds and don't disturb them, their nests, their young, or their habitat. Don't approach any closer than the birds feel comfortable with. If they alter their behavior, stop feeding, or otherwise seem agitated, back off. Obviously, if a bird flushes or flies away, you won't get a very good look anyway! Leave baby birds where you find them. When you go out bird-watching, leave your pets at home.

Use binoculars, spotting scopes, and telephoto lenses for close-up views. Make use of viewing blinds or use your vehicle as a blind. Most birds will not consider a parked vehicle as a threat, and you will get a much better view than if you get out of your car.

Don't feed birds in the wild except at backyard feeders. Never chase, herd, flush, or make deliberate noise in an attempt to get a better look, and don't alter habitat by removing rocks, branches, or natural features.

Be considerate of landowners and always ask permission to watch or photograph birds on private land. Never enter areas posted with "No Trespassing" signs without permission. On public land, observe all rules and regulations and tread lightly, staying on trails and roads. In a self-serve, fee-pay area, pay your fee instead of sneaking in. These revenues come back to all of us by supporting preservation of the habitat and public-use areas where we birders pursue our hobby!

Remember that even just watching birds has an impact. Intrusion into a bird's living space can expose it to predation, keep it from feeding or other essential activities, or cause it to leave or abandon its nest, exposing eggs or chicks to predation or the elements. No photo or viewing opportunity is worth harassing or stressing wildlife. In appreciating and watching birds and other wildlife, we have a responsibility to protect and preserve the animals that share our world.

# COMMON LOON

*Gavia immer*

**Field ID:** *Breeding plumage:* Body patterned with pearly-white squares and speckles on black; white streaking on the neck; black neck band; greenish head; red eye. *Winter plumage:* Dark gray back, nape, and crown with white throat and breast. **Size:** 32 inches.

**Habitat:** Large lakes and reservoirs.

**Field Notes:** This large waterbird has a characteristic profile in the water, riding very low so that at times much of the body is obscured and only the head and neck are easily visible. The eerie, laughing call of the loon may be renowned, but don't expect to hear it often in Colorado. Loons are not common here but do show up occasionally on deep lakes, ponds, and reservoirs around the state. In fall they are more common on the eastern plains, and there are always a few sightings in winter. Expect to see them mainly in winter plumage.

*Winter plumage*

*Podilymbus podiceps*

**Field ID:** Gray-brown with rounded head; stubby dark and white bill; short tail. **Size:** 13½ inches.

**Habitat:** Ponds, lakes, and reservoirs.

**Field Notes:** The little Pied-billed Grebe is a charming pond bird, motoring around the water's surface, then disappearing suddenly underwater only to resurface nearby. The pied-billed's small size and rapid dive have earned it the nicknames "dab-chick," "hell diver," and "water witch." Pied-billed Grebes can be found on ponds and reservoirs throughout much of the state from spring through fall. For nesting they prefer small lakes and ponds lined with cattails, to which they attach their floating nests. A few spend winter on open water areas of eastern Colorado.

*Podiceps auritus*

**Field ID:** *Breeding plumage:* Chestnut-red neck and body; dark back, wings, and head; yellow-gold "horns." *Winter plumage:* Gray with dark back, nape, and head; white cheeks and throat; "horns" have disappeared. **Size:** 13½ inches.

**Habitat:** Lakes and reservoirs.

**Field Notes:** When alarmed, the Horned Grebe, as do others of its family, sinks slowly underwater till only its head is visible, keeping watch like a periscope. When diving, it leaps forward a bit before ducking underwater. Horned Grebes are seen in Colorado mainly during spring and fall migration, and then almost entirely on reservoirs of the eastern plains. A few show up occasionally in mountain parks and western valleys. Some Horned Grebes hang around during winter on reservoirs where the water stays open.

# EARED GREBE

*Podiceps nigricollis*

**Field ID:** *Breeding plumage:* Dark with reddish wings and black neck. A fan of golden feathers above each eye leads to the name "eared." *Winter plumage:* Back, wings, head, and neck are dark gray; throat and underparts paler; "ears" have disappeared. **Size:** 12½ inches.

**Habitat:** Cattail-lined ponds and lakes; open reservoirs in winter and during migration.

**Field Notes:** Eared Grebes build floating nests of reeds and aquatic vegetation on small lakes and ponds lined with cattails—to which the grebes fasten their nests. After the young hatch, watch for them riding atop the backs of their parents. The Eared Grebe's more pointed head and longer, thinner bill help distin-

guish it from the Horned Grebe. Many Eared Grebes pass through Colorado during spring and fall migration. The ponds and lakes of North Park and the San Luis Valley host many nesting Eared Grebes in summer. Some also nest on the eastern plains.

*Winter plumage*

*Aechmophorus occidentalis*

**Field ID:** Black back, neck, and crown contrast with a white chin, throat, and undersides; yellow bill; red eye. **Size:** 25 inches.

**Habitat:** Lakes, reservoirs, and ponds.

**Field Notes:** In spring, courting pairs of Western Grebes perform an elegant dance on the lakes of Colorado. The two swim side by side, turning their faces away and back repeatedly. Swimming toward each other, they intertwine necks and pirouette slowly on the water. At the finale, the two birds rise up and together run across the water in a flurry of splashing. Western Grebes breed on vegetation-lined lakes and reservoirs in eastern Colorado and in mountain parks and western valleys, though breeding success varies with fluctuating water levels. The similar **Clark's Grebe**, once considered the same species as the western, is identical to it except the black cap starts above the eye.

*Clark's Grebe*

*family: PELICAN*

*Pelecanus erythrorhynchos*

**Field ID:** All-white bird with black wingtips; long curving neck; long orange bill equipped with a skin pouch. Except in flight or while fishing, the bill is held close to the body along the front of the neck. In flight the white pelican can be distinguished from snow geese and whooping cranes by its body shape and large size. **Size:** 62 inches; nine-foot wingspan.

**Habitat:** Large, shallow lakes; ponds, and reservoirs. They nest on islands in the middle of large lakes.

**Field Notes:** The white pelican is famous for its military behavior. These very large white birds fly in formation like an Air Force wing, landing together as if controlled by a flight commander. On the water, they fish in small groups cooperatively, forming a skirmish line and herding fish toward shallow water where they are gobbled up. Pelicans are often seen soaring very high overhead. Upwards of 10,000 pelicans may summer in Colorado. The nesting colony at Riverside Reservoir, Weld County, includes thousands of nests. Pelicans also nest at Antero Reservoir, Park County, and McFarlane Reservoir, Jackson County.

Mary Taylor Gray's Colorado Birding Tip
**Colorado Pelicans**

Pelicans in Colorado? Upwards of 10,000 American White Pelicans spend the summer in our state, mainly on the reservoirs of eastern Colorado. Many pelicans can also be found on reservoirs in South Park. In some years the state's largest pelican nesting colony, at Riverside Reservoir in Weld County, may have 2,000 nests. Any large, shallow pond or lake is likely to host pelicans. Watch for these very large white birds with black wingtips fishing together in military precision or circling high in the sky.

*Phalacrocorax auritus*

family: CORMORANT

**Field ID:** Large and black with a hooked bill; patch of bare yellow skin under the bill. Breeding adults have two feathery "crests" on the head. **Size:** 32 inches.

**Habitat:** Lakes, reservoirs, and ponds.

**Field Notes:** In flight, the cormorant looks like a black goose, but unlike the goose it flies in silence. On the water the cormorant has such a low profile it may often look like a periscope—just a long neck sticking up out of the water, its hooked bill tipped slightly up. Perched on a snag or post, the cormorant is unmistakable with its curving neck and upright pose, often with its wings held out. To reduce buoyancy for diving, cormorants lack waterproofing oils; thus cormorants must stretch their wings out to dry after diving. They nest in colonies, their stick nests usually in cottonwoods near or over water. Cormorants are abundant on the lakes and reservoirs of eastern Colorado in summer; a few remain in winter.

*Botaurus lentiginosus*

**Field ID:** Golden-brown with streaks of darker brown and buff. Black streaks down sides of long neck; pointed bill. **Size:** 28 inches.

**Habitat:** Cattail marshes and wet meadows.

**Field Notes:** The bittern has taken camouflage to new heights. If it perceives danger, this shy marsh-dweller points its bill straight up, blending into the aquatic vegetation like just another reed. To be able to keep watch even when posing as a reed, the bittern's eyes are positioned low on its cheeks. Bitterns are not common in Colorado, inhabiting wetlands along the Rio Grande and the Platte and Arkansas River drainages, as well as some mountain parks in summer. Watchers may hear the male's booming *chunk-a-lunk* call in spring.

*Ardea herodias*

**Field ID:** Large; blue-gray; long legs; long neck; spearlike bill. During breeding season it develops a long, feathery plume from the back of the head. **Size:** 46 inches.

**Habitat:** Shallow water at the edges of streams, rivers, lakes, and ponds; marshy areas.

**Field Notes:** The Great Blue Heron is a well-known and abundant wading bird in Colorado. Its slender shape poised motionless in the shallows of a pond or at the edge of a stream is a familiar sight. Great blues are found in wetland areas throughout Colorado in summer. Herons build large stick nests, usually in the upper branches of large trees at the edge of a lake, pond, or stream, often in large, colonial heronries. Some herons remain in the state through winter, particularly along the South Platte and Arkansas River drainages.

Jan Feb **Mar Apr May June July Aug Sept Oct** Nov Dec    *29*

# SNOWY EGRET

family: HERON

*Egretta thula*

**Field ID:** All white; black bill and legs; yellow feet.
**Size:** 24 inches.

**Habitat:** Edges of lakes and ponds; wet meadows, flooded farm fields, and marshes.

**Field Notes:** The Snowy Egret is a beautiful bird, looking like a small cloud puff poised at the edge of a pond or in a flooded field or wet meadow. This slender, medium-sized heron has an interesting hunting strategy. It wades through shallow water, lifting and stirring with its bright yellow feet. The idea is that prey will be startled by the flash of yellow and flush from hiding, to be grabbed by the watchful heron. Snowy Egrets are mainly migrants through Colorado, though a few stay through the summer. They are most common in eastern Colorado, particularly along the South Platte and Arkansas River drainages.

*Bubulcus ibis*

**Field ID:** White with orange bill and legs; in breeding season, orange plumes on breast and crown. **Size:** 20 inches.

**Habitat:** Wet meadows; farm fields; marshes, ponds, and lakes.

**Field Notes:** The Cattle Egret, a medium-sized white heron, is often mistaken for the similar Snowy Egret. The Cattle Egret is stockier in shape and has an orange bill and legs. True to their name, Cattle Egrets often follow stock animals, feeding on insects stirred up by the grazing animals. Cattle Egrets are originally from Africa; they showed up in North America in the 1940s, a result of natural range expansion. They were first seen in Colorado in 1964. Cattle Egrets are mainly migrants through our state, primarily in eastern Colorado.

Jan Feb **Mar Apr May June July Aug Sept** Oct Nov Dec

*family: HERON*

*Nycticorax nycticorax*

**Field ID:** Black back; gray wing and tail; white undersides; short neck and legs; red eyes; black cap with long white plumes. Immatures are a streaky yellow and brown. **Size:** 20 inches.

**Habitat:** Marshes; streamsides and river edges; lakes and reservoirs; urban and suburban ponds and waterways.

*Immature*

**Field Notes:** As evening approaches, night-herons stir from daytime roosts and fly out to feeding areas along ponds and streams. Flying in small groups, they call raucously—*quok!* They often roost motionless in the trees of parks and populated areas, looking a bit like sullen teenagers with their slouched, no-neck posture. Night-herons are seen statewide in migration. Summer colonies nest mainly in the San Luis Valley and northeastern plains. Some night-herons spend winter around the Denver metro area. The similar **Yellow-crowned Night-Heron** is occasionally seen in the state during migration.

*Yellow-crowned Night-Heron*

Mary Taylor Gray's Colorado Birding Tip
**City Park Herons**

Black-crowned Night-Herons adapt well to life around humans, as a large colony nesting in Denver's City Park proves. In summer, as many as 40 nests of night-herons, and quite a few Double-crested Cormorants, dot the trees of a small island in Ferril Lake. The herons raise their young heedless of the runners, cyclists, and mothers with strollers passing by on the shore just yards away. In evening, the skies over east Denver neighborhoods fill with night-herons as the adults wing out to the South Platte River, Cherry Creek, and other nearby waterways to feed.

*Plegadis chihi*

family: IBIS

**Field ID:** Rich bronze with green, copper, and red highlights. The glossy plumage often appears black in low light. The ibis has long legs and neck and a long, down-curved bill. In breeding season, white feathers outline its face. **Size:** 23 inches.

**Habitat:** Shorelines of ponds and reservoirs; mudflats; marshes; wet meadows; and flooded farm fields.

**Field Notes:** Ibises fly with legs held out behind and necks extended, displaying their distinctive down-curving bill. Their flight pattern is also distinguishing: Groups of ibises fly in diagonal lines, or occasional V's, alternately flapping and gliding in unison. White-faced Ibises are seen in Colorado mainly during migration, when they descend onto marsh and shoreline habitats in groups numbering from 10 to hundreds. Their numbers are greatest in spring. Some nest in the San Luis Valley at Russell and San Luis Lakes, Monte Vista and Alamosa National Wildlife Refuges, and other areas.

*Cygnus columbianus*

**Field ID:** Very large; all white; long neck; black bill; a yellow spot between the bill and eye. **Size:** 52 inches.

**Habitat:** Lakes and reservoirs.

**Field Notes:** Tundra Swans are one of several large, white waterbirds seen in Colorado. They are very large and long-necked, though lacking the curving "swan neck" of European swans. Snow Geese are much smaller than Tundra Swans (which may weigh as much as 18 pounds) and lack the swan's characteristic elegant posture. Tundra Swans can also be distinguished from white pelicans, which have very long orange bills. Tundra Swans are rare in Colorado, passing through during migration. But with their large size and elegant bearing, sighting one is always a treat. Watch for them mainly in fall on the eastern plains as well as in mountain parks and western valleys.

*Chen caerulescens*

**Field ID:** Snow-white with black wingtips; pinkish legs; black "lipstick" on the bill. The dark phase Blue Goose is blue-gray with a white head. **Size:** 28 inches.

**Habitat:** Reservoirs; wet meadows; farm fields.

**Field Notes:** Fall and winter are the seasons for Snow Geese in Colorado, when thousands of these handsome white geese flock to eastern reservoirs. A reservoir busy with geese is like Grand Central Station, with groups coming in to land or heading out to feed in surrounding fields. Snow Geese may gather by the hundreds in farm fields after harvest to feed on waste grain, particularly corn. Notice how they fly in trailing lines or in U formation, rather than the crisp V of Canada Geese. The Snow Goose's voice, which is more of a high-pitched, cacophonous honking, also differs from the Canada's two-toned honk.

*Blue Goose*

*Branta canadensis*

**Field ID:** Very large with grayish-brown plumage; long black neck; black head with white chinstrap. **Size:** 25–45 inches.

**Habitat:** Reservoirs, lakes, and ponds; grassy banks and shorelines; marshes and wet meadows; farm fields; golf courses; urban and suburban parks and open spaces.

**Field Notes:** Canada Geese are among the most familiar, visible, and abundant waterfowl in Colorado, gathering by the thousands due to our relatively mild winters and large amount of open water. They can become pests on urban and suburban lawns, golf courses, and parks. Yet few of us can resist the haunting sound of autumn "goose music" as trailing V's of Canada Geese pass overhead, honking and calling. Spring and early summer find the goose family swimming together on ponds and lakes, the long-necked parents with a line of fluffy, yellow-and-black babies trailing behind.

*Aix sponsa*

*Female*

**Field ID:** A flashy, brightly colored duck. *Male:* Iridescent green and purple head marked with white stripes and a dramatic swept-back feather crest. *Female:* Grayish-brown with a small crest, white neck; white spot around the eye. **Size:** 18½ inches.

**Habitat:** Tree-lined streams, rivers, lakes, and reservoirs.

**Field Notes:** Wood Ducks are among the most beautiful of ducks, the males strikingly marked and multicolored. These handsome ducks are also unusual in that they nest in the cavities of trees. Heavy hunting, timber-cutting, and general habitat loss brought Wood Ducks nearly to extinction by the early part of the century. Artificial nest boxes have helped increase populations. They breed in quiet wooded areas along waterways, particularly on the eastern plains but also in the Grand Valley on the Western Slope. Some remain through winter in eastern Colorado.

Mary Taylor Gray's Colorado Birding Tip
**Duck Courtship**

In winter, courting ducks put on a terrific show on Colorado lakes and waterways. Mallards raise their breasts out of the water, grunting and whistling. Great rafts of Green-winged Teal all waggle and call *krick-et*. Common Goldeneyes lay their heads on their backs, point their bills to the sky, and grunt-quack. Hooded Mergansers fan their marvelous head crests. Wigeons whistle, spout water, and point one wing to the sky.

*Anas crecca*

**Field ID:** *Male:* Gray sides showing an almost pointillist pattern; chestnut-red head with an emerald stripe down the side; yellow patch beneath the tail; white "finger" on side. *Female:* A nondescript brown. Both male and female have a characteristic green patch on the wing. **Size:** 14½ inches.

**Habitat:** Ponds and reservoirs; marshes and wet meadows.

**Field Notes:** The Green-winged Teal is remarkable for its compact size, appearing almost like a toy duckie when in close proximity to larger ducks like Mallards. In winter a pond can be covered with green-wings, the males appearing to be preening but actually enacting courtship displays. They stretch their necks, rear up a bit,

waggle their tails, fluff their wings, and give a repeated whistling call, *Krick et!* Green-winged Teal are found across the state in summer and occasionally along eastern river drainages in winter.

*Female*

*Anas platyrhynchos*

**Field ID:** *Male:* Shiny green head with white neck ring; grayish body; chestnut breast; yellow bill. *Female:* Nondescript brown. Both have purplish-blue wing patches edged in white. **Size:** 23 inches; a very large duck.

**Habitat:** Ponds, lakes, and reservoirs; streams and rivers; wetlands, marshes, and wet meadows; suburban parks and golf courses.

**Field Notes:** The green-headed Mallard is a common and very familiar duck, living statewide and showing up practically anywhere a bit of open water beckons, from streams and lakes to swimming pools and backyard ponds. Mallards are dabbling ducks, meaning they sit on the surface of shallow water and duck their heads under to reach aquatic plants, insects, and detritus in the mud. It is a common sight to see a group of them tipped "bottoms-up," their feathery duck rumps all pointing toward the sky. Hundreds of thousands of Mallards pass through Colorado during migration, and thousands stay through winter.

*Female*

family: DUCK and GOOSE

*Anas acuta*

**Field ID:** *Male:* Bronze-brown body; solid brown head with a white stripe on the side, extending down the underside of the neck. Long black feathers protrude from the tail. *Female:* Drab mottled brown; lacking the exaggerated pintail. **Size:** *M:* 26 inches; *F:* 20 inches.

**Habitat:** Ponds, lakes, and reservoirs; rivers and streams; farm fields and wet meadows.

**Field Notes:** Pintails are second only to Mallards as the most common North American duck. Whether you see only a handful of pintails or a lake literally covered with a raft of them, they are always a pleasure to watch, bobbing gracefully with their arrow tails held high. Pintail females may nest far from water in a farm field or grassland. If a predator draws too near her nest, she may lure it away by feigning injury like a Killdeer. Found statewide during migration, pintails are more common on the Western Slope during summer.

*Female*

**Jan Feb Mar Apr May June July Aug Sept Oct Nov Dec**

*Anas discors*

**Field ID:** *Male:* Mottled; brownish-gray with black tail and a bold white crescent behind the bill. *Female:* A nondescript brown. The powder-blue wing patch is very noticeable on both in flight. **Size:** 15½ inches.

**Habitat:** Lakes, reservoirs and ponds; marshes, wet meadows, and farm fields.

**Field Notes:** Blue-winged Teal are dabbling ducks, but unlike Mallards that feed "bottoms-up," blue-wings skim the water with their flat bills or reach below the surface in the shallows to feed on the pond bottom. Blue-wings fly in compact, tight-turning flocks, rushing back and forth above a prospective landing site until satisfied it is safe to land, then lighting suddenly on the water as a group. In flight the powder-blue wing patch of this trim little duck flashes like a patch of sky. Blue-wings nest throughout the state in summer and are common migrants.

*Female*

*Anas cyanoptera*

**Field ID:** *Male:* Gleaming, cinnamon-red with dark back and wings. *Female:* A nondescript, scalloped brown—almost indistinguishable from other teal species. Both have green and blue patches on the wings. **Size:** 16 inches.

**Habitat:** Lakes, ponds, and reservoirs; streams and rivers; farm fields and grasslands; marshes and wet meadows.

**Field Notes:** The male Cinnamon Teal is a beautiful duck, gleaming a marvelous coppery-red in the sun. A small dabbling duck, the Cinnamon Teal is shyer in its habits than its cousins, the Mallard and Blue-winged Teal. While the Mallard has adapted well to human neighbors, the Cinnamon Teal is less tolerant of human encroachment, and its populations have declined with development and the draining of wetlands. Cinnamon Teal aren't usually seen in large flocks, preferring instead to travel in pairs. They are found statewide spring through fall.

*Female*

*Anas clypeata*

**Field ID:** *Male:* Chestnut sides with gray wings; white breast; green head. The long bill is spatulate at the end. *Female:* Mottled brown. **Size:** 19 inches.

**Habitat:** Lakes, ponds, and reservoirs; streams and rivers; farm fields and grasslands; marshes and wet meadows.

**Field Notes:** Once you get a good look at a shoveler, even the rather nondescript female, you won't mistake it for any other duck. The shoveler's long bill ends in a broad spoon shape, making it look a bit like a cartoon duck. The bill is actually wonderfully adapted to dabble tiny bits of food from the water. Despite their ungainly appearance, shovelers are good fliers and when startled rise up suddenly from the water and dart off in quick, erratic flight. Once calmed they often settle back to the spot from which they were flushed. Shovelers nest over much of the state from the Front Range westward, as well as along the South Platte and Arkansas Rivers. Some spend winter along these river drainages.

*Female*

*Anas strepera*

**Field ID:** The Gadwall is one of the least showy ducks. *Male:* Grayish with a light-brown head; black rump and tail. *Female:* A nondescript brown. The white wing patch, or speculum, is often visible along the sides on both male and female. **Size:** 20 inches.

**Habitat:** Lakes, ponds, and reservoirs; farm fields and grasslands; marshes and wet meadows.

**Field Notes:** Just when you expect all male ducks to be colorful or distinctive in some way, along comes the Gadwall. To the inattentive eye, the Gadwall is just one more gray-brown duck. Look for the black rump, with a white patch visible on the folded wings along the side. Gadwalls are found through much of the state during migration. They nest in mountain parks and valleys of the Western Slope and along the South Platte and Arkansas River drainages in the east. Some winter in the San Luis Valley and in eastern Colorado.

Mary Taylor Gray's Colorado Birding Tip
**Wintering Waterfowl**

Winter is a wonderful time to view waterfowl on the reservoirs and waterways of eastern Colorado. Sufficient ice-free water attracts an abundance of ducks, including Mallards, Gadwalls, wigeons, shovelers, pintails, Common and Hooded Mergansers, Bufflehead, Wood Ducks, Green-winged Teal, Lesser Scaup, Common Goldeneye, and occasional scoters and Oldsquaw; Tundra Swans and Canada, Lesser White-fronted, and Snow Geese, which number in the tens of thousands. Good waterfowl viewing can be found at Hamilton Reservoir near Fort Collins, John Martin Reservoir near Lamar, Bonny Reservoir along the Republican River, along Clear Creek in the Denver metro area, and all along the South Platte River, including where it passes through Denver.

*Anas americana*

**Field ID:** *Male:* Pinkish-beige with mottled gray head; iridescent-green eye stripe; white bar from bill across top of head; blue bill. *Female:* Similar to male, but lacks green eye stripe and white forehead. **Size:** 19 inches.

**Habitat:** Lakes, ponds, and reservoirs; marshes, streams, and rivers; suburban parks.

**Field Notes:** The white forehead of the male wigeon is distinctive, particularly in a mixed flock of ducks, often seeming to flash in the light as he turns his head. Wigeons are common in mountain parks and western valleys in summer, particularly at Browns Park National Wildlife Refuge and less so in North Park. Some winter along the South Platte and Arkansas River valleys and in the San Luis Valley.

*Female*

*Aythya valisineria*

**Field ID:** *Male:* Grayish-white back and sides with black breast and tail; red head and neck; long sloping bill. *Female:* Brownish-gray with sandy-brown head and neck. **Size:** 21 inches.

**Habitat:** Lakes, ponds, and reservoirs; marshes.

**Field Notes:** The Canvasback is a large duck distinguished by bold blocks of color, particularly the chestnut-red head with the long, sloped bill that gives it an aristocratic profile. The long bill helps distinguish the Canvasback from the similarly colored Redhead, which has a more typical duck-shaped profile. Named for the dotted and lined pattern on its back that resembles canvas, the Canvasback is a favorite of duck hunters. Canvasback populations have declined greatly in North America. Not common in Colorado, it passes through major river drainages during migration. A few spend summer in North Park, the San Luis Valley, and at Browns Park National Wildlife Refuge.

*Female*

*Aythya americana*

**Field ID:** *Male:* Gray body; black chest and tail contrast with the large, round, chestnut-red head. The bill is blue with a black tip. *Female:* An unremarkable brown with darker crown and pale patch on bill. **Size:** 19 inches.

**Habitat:** Lakes, ponds, and reservoirs; marshes.

**Field Notes:** Both the Redhead and the Canvasback are black and white with reddish heads, but the Redhead's large, rounded head and rounded bill distinguish it from the slope-billed Canvasback. Telling the two apart is not much of a challenge in Colorado, since the Redhead is much more common. Redheads are quite abundant through much of the state during migration and common in summer along the South Platte and Arkansas River drainages; on the Western Slope, especially in North Park; the San Luis Valley; and at Browns Park National Wildlife Refuge.

*Female*

Jan **Feb Mar Apr** May June July Aug Sept **Oct** Nov Dec

*family: DUCK and GOOSE*

## Aythya collaris

**Field ID:** *Male:* Black with gray-white sides and a white triangle on both sides; white at base of bill; head feathers slightly bumped-up. A faint brown neck ring is discernible only in good light. *Female:* Grayish-brown. Both have gray bills with a white band near the tip. **Size:** 17 inches.

**Habitat:** Lakes, ponds, and reservoirs.

**Field Notes:** The Ring-necked Duck might better be called the "ringbill," since the white stripe on its bill is much more evident than the almost invisible cinnamon-brown ring around the neck. Ring-necked Ducks are mainly seen in Colorado during migration—on the eastern plains and through parks and valleys of the Western Slope. A fair number nest near mountain lakes, beaver

ponds, and high-altitude wetlands, particularly in the north-central part of the state. Groups of wintering ring-necks often show up along the South Platte River drainage.

*Female*

**Jan Feb Mar Apr May June July Aug Sept Oct Nov Dec**

*Aythya affinis*

**Field ID:** *Male:* Head, breast, and rump black; body and back grayish-white; head slightly bumped-up; blue bill. *Female:* Brown with bumped-up head and striking white crescent behind bill.
**Size:** 16½ inches.

**Habitat:** Ponds and reservoirs; marshes.

**Field Notes:** The Lesser Scaup is very similar to the Ring-necked Duck. Both are colored in blocks of black and white, but the scaup has a gray rather than a black back and lacks the white triangles on the sides. Hunters have long nicknamed the scaup "bluebill." Lesser Scaup are common summer visitors to mountain parks, particularly North and South Parks. They pass through the state in abundance during migration, showing up in valleys, mountain parks, and on the eastern plains. Some hang around in winter, particularly along the South Platte and Arkansas River drainages.

*Female*

**Jan Feb Mar Apr May June July Aug Sept Oct Nov Dec**     *49*

# COMMON GOLDENEYE

*Bucephala clangula*

**Field ID:** *Male:* White with dark back; greenish-black head; yellow eye; prominent white spot behind the bill. *Female:* Grayish with white collar and reddish-brown head. **Size:** 18½ inches.

**Habitat:** Ponds and reservoirs; rivers.

**Field Notes:** Sometimes called "whistler" for the noise its wings make in flight, the goldeneye is remarkable more for its behavior than appearance. Winter is courtship time for ducks, and the male

goldeneye puts on quite a show. Swimming near a female, he suddenly throws his head back until his bill points to the sky. Uttering a grunting, nasal quack—*Brrrt!*—he kicks his legs back with a splash. Goldeneyes are common winter visitors to Colorado wherever open water beckons.

*Female*

family: DUCK and GOOSE

**Jan Feb Mar** Apr May June July Aug Sept Oct **Nov Dec**

*Bucephala albeola*

**Field ID:** *Male:* White with black back; large, black head with prominent white patch. *Female:* Grayish with darker head; oblong white patch behind eye that is smaller than white patch on male's head. **Size:** 13½ inches.

**Habitat:** Reservoirs, ponds, mountain beaver ponds, and "kettle" ponds.

**Field Notes:** The bubble-headed Bufflehead is well named. Its genus name, *bucephala*, in fact means "buffalo-head." Buffleheads are among those odd-seeming ducks that nest in holes in trees. Woodpecker cavities in old aspen trees at the edges of mountain wetlands, beaver ponds, and glacial-carved kettle ponds provide good nesting habitat for them. Buffleheads are fairly common throughout western parks and valleys and on the eastern plains during migration. They nest infrequently near high-mountain ponds, particularly at the kettle lakes (Hidden, Teal, Big Creek) on the east side of the Mount Zirkel Wilderness above North Park.

*Female*

*Lophodytes cucullatus*

**Field ID:** *Male:* Rusty-brown sides with black back; fan-shaped black head with prominent white patch; thin, short bill. *Female:* Pale gray-brown with darker back; reddish fan-shaped crest; thin bill. **Size:** 18 inches.

**Habitat:** Lakes, ponds, and reservoirs; rivers.

**Field Notes:** The male Hooded Merganser is quite an eye-opener when seen in full sail with his oversized head crest fanned out. The elevated crest with the white patch boldly exposed actually means the male is agitated or displaying for a female. When calm, his crest is folded smoothly down. The Hooded Merganser is quite a bit smaller than other mergansers, with head and bill that seem particularly smaller. Winter is the best time to see them

along the rivers and reservoirs of eastern Colorado and in the valleys and mountain parks of the west.

*Female*

*Mergus merganser*

**Field ID:** *Male:* Snowy-white with black back; greenish-black head; red-orange bill. *Female:* Grayish with white breast and chin; reddish head with ragged, backward-pointing crest.
**Size:** 25 inches.

**Habitat:** Reservoirs; rivers.

**Field Notes:** Diving ducks, mergansers use their specialized narrow, pointed bills with serrated edges to hold on to their slippery fish prey. The bottom edge of the lower bill is characteristically flat and straight. The Common Merganser is large and almost goose-sized; in Britain mergansers are called "goosanders," which means "goose-duck." Winter is the best time for Common Mergansers in Colorado, when they sail the rivers and reservoirs of eastern Colorado, western valleys, and mountain parks. Some spend summer along rivers of the San Luis Valley; western mountains; and North, Middle, and South Parks.

*Female*

*Mergus serrator*

**Field ID:** *Male:* Speckled gray with black back; rusty-red breast; white neck ring; green head with a rough crest. *Female:* Gray-brown with rusty head and tattered-looking crest.
**Size:** 23 inches.

**Habitat:** Reservoirs; rivers.

**Field Notes:** The Red-breasted Merganser can be distinguished from the common by its streaked breast and raggedy green crest. Because of its reddish breast, this duck is sometimes called the sea robin. Red-breasted Mergansers are much less common in Colorado than Common Mergansers, passing through eastern Colorado and some western valleys during migration, a few staying to winter on the eastern plains near the Front Range.

*Female*

*Oxyura jamaicensis*

**Field ID:** *Male:* Cinnamon colored; blue bill; two-toned head—black above the eye line and white below. In winter colored body and bill fade to charcoal gray. *Female:* Dark brown; less dramatically two-toned head—dark down to the eye line and paler below. **Size:** 15 inches.

**Habitat:** Ponds and reservoirs; marshes.

**Field Notes:** Charming little ducks, ruddies sail about quiet ponds and marshes like bobbing toys. The males are nicknamed "stiff-tails" for their habit of holding their long, wedge-shaped tails cocked up. The ruddy's plumage and bill are so strongly colored in summer that the transformation to dull winter plumage is quite striking. In summer they are fairly common in mountain parks and valleys, particularly the San Luis Valley, North Park, and Browns Park National Wildlife Refuge. They also show up occasionally in winter in western valleys and on the eastern plains near the mountains.

*Female*

Jan Feb Mar **Apr May June July Aug Sept Oct Nov** Dec

# TURKEY VULTURE

*Cathartes aura*

**Field ID:** Large, black, and hawklike; very large, broad wings; naked red head. **Size:** 27 inches; six-foot wingspan.

**Habitat:** Grasslands; shrublands; farm fields and open country; nesting in steep, rocky terrain and cliffs near open land.

**Field Notes:** Overhead, the Turkey Vulture can be differentiated from a hawk by its smaller head, lighter trailing edges of the wings, and the way it holds its wings up slightly in a V,

rocking slightly side to side as it soars. Vultures are most often seen soaring endlessly on thermal air currents, high in the sky. They may also be spotted roosting in trees, particularly during migration. By scavenging on dead animals, vultures play an essential role in the ecosystem, helping recycle nutrients locked up in the bodies of other animals. Vultures were recently reclassified as being more closely related to the stork family than to the birds of prey.

*Pandion haliaetus*

**Field ID:** Charcoal back and wings and white undersides. The white head has a crest of trailing feathers and a horizontal black stripe through the eyes. In flight, black wrist patches are evident. **Size:** 22–25 inches.

**Habitat:** Lakes, reservoirs, and large ponds.

**Field Notes:** This beautifully marked bird of prey, a specialist that lives almost exclusively on fish, hunts open waters with a fierce and watchful eye, striking with great power and speed once it spots a silvery body in the water below. As have Bald Eagles and Peregrine Falcons, Osprey populations suffered from DDT poisoning as well as from loss of their wetlands habitat. Fortunately, Osprey are making a recovery after strong conservation efforts, including the banning of DDT. In summer, they inhabit lakes and reservoirs in the mountains, particularly in Grand County, and occasionally in eastern Colorado.

Mary Taylor Gray's Colorado Birding Tip
**Osprey Hot Spot**

With their large size and dramatic hunting style, Osprey are a magnificent raptor to watch. About 20 active Osprey nests on Shadow Mountain Reservoir and Lake Granby in Grand County provide good summer viewing of these fish-eating hawks and their hunting and nesting behavior. Watchers can rent canoes to get closer views, but must keep off the nesting islands, which are closed from May 1 to September 1 to protect the Osprey, and should avoid boating right under the trees, which might stress the birds.

Jan Feb Mar **Apr May June July Aug Sept Oct** Nov Dec

# BALD EAGLE

*Haliaeetus leucocephalus*

family: HAWK

**Field ID:** Dark brown plumage with snowy white head and tail; yellow beak; unfeathered yellow legs and talons. Immature birds lack the white head and have mottled white markings on the tail and underparts. Immature Bald Eagles are often mistaken for Golden Eagles. **Size:** 31–37 inches.

**Habitat:** Rivers; lakes and reservoirs; open water, and open country around prairie dog towns.

**Field Notes:** Bald Eagles make quite a sight in winter among the bare cottonwoods along a river or reservoir, their white heads dotting the branches like ornaments. In 1997 there were 29 known Bald Eagle nest sites in the state. The breeding birds remain in Colorado year-round. Be sure to avoid disturbing any nests or nesting adults you might be aware of. Bald Eagles suffered severely from DDT poisoning, shooting, and habitat loss. Previously endangered, their numbers have improved significantly after decades of conservation efforts and they are now classified as a threatened species.

Mary Taylor Gray's Colorado Birding Tip
### Wintering Eagles

Up to 1,200 Bald Eagles winter in Colorado, attracted by our relatively mild winters and abundance of waterfowl and prairie dogs. The Rocky Mountain Arsenal National Wildlife Refuge offers the best eagle-viewing in the Denver metro area. The Swallows Watchable Wildlife Site at Pueblo Reservoir, Jackson Reservoir in Weld County, and John Martin Reservoir near Lamar are good eastern Colorado eagle-viewing sites. On the Western Slope, eagles winter along the White, Colorado, and Yampa Rivers.

**Jan Feb** Mar Apr May June July Aug Sept Oct **Nov Dec**

*Aquila chrysaetos*

**family: HAWK**

**Field ID:** Rich, dark brown with a light golden wash over head and nape. Unlike the Bald Eagle, the golden's legs are feathered down to the feet. Beak and head are smaller than the Bald Eagle, but the tail is longer. Immature birds have a white tail with a dark terminal band. **Size:** 30–40 inches.

**Habitat:** Grasslands; shrublands; pine forests; cliffs and canyons at the edge of open country.

**Field Notes:** With its very large size and uniform dark appearance, a Golden Eagle shouldn't be mistaken for any of the large, dark hawks. In flight it is impressive, its wingspan spreading seven feet or more, with wings often tipped slightly up. Golden Eagles are more common in Colorado in the winter and distributed statewide. There are an estimated 600–900 active Golden Eagle nests in the state, concentrated in northwestern Colorado. Golden Eagles choose cliff nesting sites on the edge of open country, where they hunt for small mammals and other prey.

# MISSISSIPPI KITE

family: HAWK

*Ictinia mississippiensis*

CATHY AND GORDON ILLG

**Field ID:** Dark gray with lighter gray head and undersides; long pointed wings; long black squared-off tail; red eye. Immature is a streaky brown. **Size:** 14½ inches.

**Habitat:** Riparian areas and urban parks along the Arkansas River drainage.

**Field Notes:** The name "kite" might make you ponder whether the bird or the toy was named first. In fact, the soaring toy-on-a-string was named for the way its twisting and diving motion in the air mimics the graceful, acrobatic flight of these small raptors, which wheel, dive, and glide pursuing insects in the air. Colorado represents the northern edge of the Mississippi Kite's range. They are found in our state only, very locally, along the Arkansas River Valley in eastern Colorado.

Mary Taylor Gray's Colorado Birding Tip
**Mississippi Kites**

Colorado is at the northern tip of the range of a handsome raptor, the Mississippi Kite. The only kite seen regularly in our state, it has moved into Colorado along the wooded corridor of the Arkansas River. The best place to spot these sleek gray birds is in Willow Creek Park in Lamar, where a number of kites nest each summer. They can be seen flying about the park feeding on cicadas and other insects.

*Circus cyaneus*

CORNELL LABORATORY OF ORNITHOLOGY

**Field ID:** Slender body; long tail; tapered wings; white rump; stripes around the long tail; a dish-shaped ruff of feathers framing the face. *Male:* Blue-gray with black wingtips and whitish underparts. *Female:* Brown with streaked, whitish underparts. Female is larger than the male. Immatures resemble females. **Size:** *M:* 17 inches; *F:* 23 inches.

**Habitat:** Marshes; wetlands; grasslands; farm fields and pastures; road edges.

**Field Notes:** Formerly called the marsh hawk, the harrier is a common and familiar bird of wetlands and grasslands. The harrier flies close above the ground, listening and watching for prey below. As it courses on wings tipped up in a V, the harrier teeters slightly side to side. Its white rump is distinctive. Harriers are so-named because they "harry" their prey, dropping toward the ground as they hunt to startle small mammals from hiding. Harriers are found throughout the state from spring through fall, and in the eastern half of the state in winter.

# SHARP-SHINNED HAWK

*Accipiter striatus*

**Field ID:** Adults have a barred, reddish breast; steel-gray back; red eye. Immatures are brown with streaky red-brown underparts. **Size:** 11 inches.

**Habitat:** Forests and woodlands including coniferous forests; riparian areas; urban and suburban parks and yards.

**Field Notes:** Sharp-shinned Hawks, nicknamed "sharpshins" or "sharpies" by birders, belong to a group of woodland hawks called accipiters. Adapted to life among the trees, they have short, rounded wings and long, banded tails. Sharpies are bird-eaters and have discovered backyard bird feeders to be productive hunting grounds, much to the horror of many homeowners. Their flight pattern is a series of short flaps followed by a glide. The sharpie's tail is squared at the bottom, not rounded like a Cooper's Hawk.

*Accipiter cooperii*

**Field ID:** Slate-blue with barred reddish breast; banded tail; red eye. Immature is brown with reddish-streaked under-parts. **Size:** 16 inches.

**Habitat:** Forests and woodlands including coniferous forests; riparian areas; urban and suburban parks and yards; agricul-tural land and grasslands with adjacent trees.

**Field Notes:** Differentiating between a Sharp-shinned and Cooper's Hawk is a chal-lenge even to many seasoned birders. Both inhabit wooded areas; have short, rounded wings; long, banded tails; and hunt birds. The Cooper's is larger (though a large female sharpie is as big as a small male Cooper's), has a tail rounded at the end and a larger head, and the crown is much darker, almost black, compared with the body. Cooper's Hawks prefer coniferous forests for breeding.

family: HAWK

Mary Taylor Gray's Colorado Birding Tip
**Dakota Hogback Hawkwatch**

The top spot in Colorado to view migrating raptors is just west of Denver, the Dakota Hogback Hawkwatch. Spring offers the best viewing, with more than 5,000 birds sometimes counted. Most numerous are Red-tailed Hawks, followed by American Kestrels and Turkey Vultures. Other species include Ferruginous, Sharp-shinned, Cooper's, Swainson's, and Broad-winged Hawks, as well as harriers, Osprey, Bald and Golden Eagles, Merlins, and Prairie and Peregrine Falcons. From the RTD Park & Ride at I-70 and Colorado 26, walk up an old road northeast to a signed trail, then about one-half mile to the Hawkwatch site by the three power poles on the ridge summit.

# NORTHERN GOSHAWK

*Accipiter gentilis*

**Field ID:** Blue-gray; grayish-white underparts barred with gray; long tail with dark bands; fluffy white undertail feathers. Head is paler with a black cap and white eyebrow. Immature is dark brown with streaked buffy underparts. **Size:** 21–26 inches.

**Habitat:** Mountain forests, particularly ponderosa and lodge-pole pine, as well as aspen; riparian areas and lower elevations in winter and during migration.

**Field Notes:** The goshawk prefers mature pine forests. Thought to be uncommon in Colorado, goshawks may be more plentiful than we realize. Inhabiting dense coniferous forests, the goshawk is the largest of the accipiter group of woodland hawks. It flies on large powerful wings, its wingstrokes deep and strong as opposed to the *flap-flap-glide* pattern of Cooper's and Sharp-shinned Hawks. Its wings are longer and tail shorter in proportion to the body than the other accipiters, and it eats mainly mammals instead of birds.

*Buteo swainsoni*

RUSSELL BURDEN

**Field ID:** Dark head, back, and wings; light breast and undersides; white chin; reddish-brown bib across the neck and upper chest. In flight, the wing linings are lighter than the trailing flight feathers. **Size:** 21 inches.

**Habitat:** Prairies and grasslands; farm fields and pastures; shrublands; riparian areas.

**Field Notes:** The coppery-brown cowl that extends to midbreast identifies the Swainson's Hawk. These large, handsome hawks hunt open country, particularly the grasslands and agricultural land of eastern Colorado. Though you might think they eat mice, rabbits, and small mammals, their primary prey is grasshoppers and insects. They are often seen perched on power poles along country roads. Come fall, these hawks migrate thousands of miles south to spend winter in Argentina.

Mary Taylor Gray's Colorado Birding Tip
**Winter Hawk/Summer Hawk**

Spring and fall signal something of a changing of the guard among Colorado's birds of prey. Our primary summer hawk, the Swainson's, migrates thousands of miles from Argentina to nest in eastern Colorado. By contrast, the arctic-nesting Rough-Legged Hawk is a common winter hawk, especially on the eastern plains. Though Ferruginous Hawks inhabit our state year-round, their numbers swell in winter with the arrival of migrants from the north, attracted by Colorado's prairie dog populations.

# RED-TAILED HAWK

*Buteo jamaicensis*

**Field ID:** Reddish-brown with a streaked, creamy breast; speckled, reddish belly band; characteristic rusty-red tail. Two other color phases—an almost solid dark brown and a pale form with head and tail almost white—make identification confusing. These forms are not common in Colorado. Immature hawks lack the red tail. **Size:** 22 inches.

**Habitat:** Grasslands; farm fields and pastures; riparian areas; forests.

**Field Notes:** The most abundant, widespread, and familiar hawk of the West, the Red-tailed Hawk resides year-round in Colorado. Adult birds are readily identified by their rusty-red tail. Dark bars along the undersides of the leading edge of the outstretched wings, near the shoulder, are also characteristic. We often see redtails perched on power poles or soaring in the air on broad wings, carving slow, wide arcs. The redtail's dramatic call fits its image as a western icon. The down-slurred scream—*Keeeer!*—is often heard as a background sound in movies and television shows.

**Jan Feb Mar Apr May June July Aug Sept Oct Nov Dec**

*Buteo regalis*

family: HAWK

**Field ID:** Reddish-brown back; pale head; underside streaked with rufous-red. A dark V formed by the brown, fully feathered legs against the white body is visible in flight. The rare dark phase is reddish brown all over. **Size:** 23 inches.

**Habitat:** Grasslands and sagebrush shrublands.

**Field Notes:** The Ferruginous Hawk's decline in numbers, due to the development of the prairies, has biologists worried. A true grassland hawk, the "ferrug," as it is often nicknamed, is a consummate prairie dog hunter; thus 'dog towns are good places to look for them. Some Ferruginous Hawks nest in Colorado, but an influx of hawks in the winter, particularly to eastern Colorado, leads many to consider the ferrug a winter hawk in our state.

**Jan Feb Mar** Apr May June July Aug Sept Oct **Nov Dec**        *67*

# ROUGH-LEGGED HAWK

*Buteo lagopus*

**Field ID:** There are two color phases of the roughleg. The light phase has a pale, speckled body; darker back and belly band; characteristic black wrist patches visible on the open wings; dark band at the tip of the white tail. The dark phase is uniformly dark with lighter flight feathers edged in dark. Legs of all birds are feathered to the toes. **Size:** 22 inches.

**Habitat:** Grasslands; shrublands; farm fields and pastures; riparian areas.

**Field Notes:** A winter hawk in Colorado, Rough-legged Hawks' numbers peak in December and January, particularly in eastern Colorado. Roughlegs nest in the far north at the edge of the arctic tree line, migrating south to spend winter in Colorado's relatively moderate climate. Challenging to identify, Rough-legged Hawks have various plumages and are close in size and shape to other large broad-winged hawks, such as redtails and Ferruginous Hawks.

*Falco sparverius*

**family: FALCON**

**Field ID:** *Male:* Rusty-red back with black barring; peach breast with streaky spotting; blue-gray wings; red tail. The crown of the head is blue-gray with a reddish spot. *Female:* Resembles the male though her wings are rusty-brown and she is larger than the male. Both sexes have two vertical black stripes or "whiskers" down the cheeks; large eyes; and short, hooked bill. **Size:** 12 inches.

**Habitat:** Fields; grasslands; roadsides; urban and suburban parks and gardens.

**Field Notes:** The kestrel combines beauty and grace in form and motion, all in a package not much larger than a robin. The smallest of North American raptors (excluding owls), the kestrel is also among the most common. Adapted well to life around humans, it may show up in almost any habitat in the state. Nicknamed sparrow hawks because they were once flown at sparrows by falconers, kestrels actually feed mainly on grasshoppers and small mammals. The similar **Merlin** is slightly larger than the kestrel, with less prominent facial whiskers. The male is gray-blue and the female brown, both with streaked breasts. Merlins are seen in Colorado mainly during migration.

*Female*                                                                  *Merlin*

*Falco mexicanus*

**family: FALCON**

**Field ID:** Pale brown with a creamy breast streaked and spotted with brown. Two facial "whiskers" on each cheek are much more slender than the facial marks on a Peregrine Falcon. In flight, dark "armpits" and wing linings contrast with the pale body. **Size:** 15½–19½ inches.

**Habitat:** Grasslands; fields and pastures; shrublands; tundra; nesting in cliffs adjacent to open country.

**Field Notes:** Interesting members of their family, Prairie Falcons sometimes seem more like hawks than falcons. They nest on cliffs and hunt over open country, seeking small mammals and birds. While Peregrine Falcons plummet down upon their prey, Prairie Falcons catch most of their meals on or close to the ground, using lightning speed and maneuverability. They also fly low over the ground, flushing small birds, which they quickly pursue and grab from midair. Prairie Falcons live year-round in Colorado and are found statewide.

*Falco peregrinus*

**Immature**

**family: FALCON**

**Field ID:** Slate-blue back and wings; pale undersides with dark barring. The head has a blue helmet with a wide bar or "sideburn" on the cheek. The tail is long and the wings are tapering and pointed. **Size:** 16–21 inches.

**Habitat:** Cliffs and canyons; urban areas with tall buildings; coniferous forests; reservoirs and wetlands during migration and in winter.

**Field Notes:** In the mid-seventies, only four pairs of Peregrine Falcons nested in Colorado. Through the 1980s, 500 young peregrines were carefully hatched in captivity and released to the wild. In 1997, researchers counted 89 occupied nest sites in our state, far beyond the original target of 20 active nests. The peregrine, presently a threatened species in Colorado, is seen in our state in summer and during migration.

Mary Taylor Gray's Colorado Birding Tip
**The Comeback Falcon**

With diligent recovery efforts from biologists and conservationists, the Peregrine Falcon has made a remarkable comeback, both nationally and in Colorado. Nearly vanished 20 years ago, today peregrines can be seen in many places—Mesa Verde National Park, Black Canyon of the Gunnison, Colorado and Dinosaur National Monuments, Chimney Rock near Pagosa Springs, the Flatirons and rocky foothills west of Boulder, and even downtown Denver, where they have been spotted roosting atop Coors Field.

Jan Feb Mar **Apr May June July Aug Sept Oct** Nov Dec

*family: GROUSE and PTARMIGAN*

*Phasianus colchicus*

**Field ID:** *Male:* Plump, golden body mottled with black; long plumed tail; small greenish-black head set on a slender white-banded neck. The eyes are surrounded by circles of naked red skin; the head has two small feathery tufts. *Female:* Smaller and duller than the male, brown with a shorter tail.
**Size:** *M:* 33 inches; *F:* 21 inches.

**Habitat:** Fields; grasslands; agricultural areas.

**Field Notes:** With his emerald head and sweeping gold and black tail, the pheasant cock appears like a richly dressed sultan among the drab brown females. Flushed from the ground, the pheasant takes off in a whir, its plump body sailing just above the vegetation on short wings before landing again at a safe distance. Though a very common bird of fields and grasslands and a favorite of bird hunters, Ring-necked Pheasants are not native to Colorado. A Chinese species, they were first introduced into Colorado in 1894 as game birds. Pheasants are year-round residents of agricultural land of the eastern plains as well as the San Luis Valley and Western Slope valleys.

CORNELL LABORATORY OF ORNITHOLOGY

*Female*

**Jan Feb Mar Apr May June July Aug Sept Oct Nov Dec**

*Dendragapus obscurus*

CORNELL LABORATORY OF ORNITHOLOGY

**Field ID:** *Male:* Blue-gray with plump body; long neck; smallish head; orange-yellow comb above the eye.
*Female:* Mottled brown with paler underparts. **Size:** 20 inches.

**Habitat:** Mountain coniferous and aspen forests.

**Field Notes:** Many hikers in Colorado's montane and subalpine forests have made the surprising acquaintance of Blue Grouse as the birds perched in trees or marched along on the ground in close proximity. Blue Grouse often seem unafraid of humans. Because of their docile nature and habit of freezing in

the trees and relying on protective coloration instead of flying off, they have been nicknamed "fool grouse." Blue Grouse are primarily ground-dwelling in the summer, but in winter roost in coniferous trees.

***Female***

family: GROUSE and PTARMIGAN

*Lagopus leucurus*

CORNELL LABORATORY OF ORNITHOLOGY

**Field ID:** *Winter plumage:* Snow white. *Summer plumage:* Mottled brown with white underparts. A plump-bodied, small-headed grouse.
**Size:** 12½ inches.

**Habitat:** Alpine tundra, particularly willow thickets in winter.

**Field Notes:** So wonderfully camouflaged are ptarmigan that hikers often don't see them, or spot them only as the birds flush, practically from underfoot, fluttering off across the tundra to settle a safe distance away. Ptarmigan are mottled brown in summer, making them indistinguishable against a backdrop of rocky tundra, and gradually turn white with the coming of the snow. By winter their plumage is snow-white. Feathery "snowshoes" on their feet help them get around on the snow.

Mary Taylor Gray's Colorado Birding Tip
## Ptarmigan of the Tundra

The White-tailed Ptarmigan mirrors the seasons above timberline. A mottled brown that blends with the landscape in summer, the ptarmigan turns snowy white in winter. The best places to view this tundra-dweller are the basins around Guanella Pass above Georgetown, Trail Ridge Road in Rocky Mountain National Park, and Summit Lake on Mount Evans. You may not see these secretive birds until you have practically stepped on them.

**Jan Feb Mar Apr May June July Aug Sept Oct Nov Dec**

*Centrocercus urophasianus*

**Field ID:** *Male:* Large and plump with streaky gray-brown plumage; black belly; long tail; prominent white ruff and collar; yellow combs over the eyes; black throat. *Female:* Smaller than male; lacks eye combs, neck ruff, and collar. **Size:** 28 inches.

**Habitat:** Sagebrush shrublands.

family: GROUSE and PTARMIGAN

**Field Notes:** True to their name, Sage Grouse inhabit western Colorado shrublands dominated by big sagebrush. Sage Grouse feed on the aromatic leaves and buds of sagebrush, shelter beneath it, and build their nests in its cover. Lewis and Clark shot a number of these grouse, calling them "the cock of the plains," but found them to be unpalatable, the meat strongly flavored from the sagebrush that was the birds' primary food. Sage Grouse are year-round residents primarily in the northwestern part of the state, North and Middle Parks, and in Gunnison County. Sage Grouse are much larger than other grouse, quail, and prairie-chickens.

Mary Taylor Gray's Colorado Birding Tip
### Spring Dancers

On the sagebrush flats of mountain parks, male Sage Grouse perform their stylized courtship dance, strutting and inflating the enormous air sacs on their throats, then forcing the air out with a pop. Several leks, or traditional dancing grounds, in North Park are accessible to the public, but it is imperative visitors behave responsibly at these sites, which are critical to this species' reproductive success. Arrive before dawn, being very careful not to drive onto the lek. Stay in cars, keep very quiet, and don't leave until the birds are off the lek, usually by midmorning. Directions to the sites, and rules and ethics for viewing, are available through the Walden Chamber of Commerce, 970-723-4600.

**Jan Feb Mar Apr May June July Aug Sept Oct Nov Dec**

*family: GROUSE and PTARMIGAN*

## *Tympanuchus cupido*

**Field ID:** Mottled buffy and brown plumage with black barring; paler undersides with brown barring; yellow comb over eyes. *Male:* Yellow-orange neck sacs and ornamental neck feathers erected like horns during courtship.
**Size:** 17 inches.

**Habitat:** Sand prairie and rangeland of sandhill country, and adjacent agricultural land.

D. ROBERT FRANZ

**Field Notes:** The prairie-chicken indeed looks like its namesake if you should happen to see one scurrying for cover or flying (briefly) alongside a country road. A threatened species in Colorado, the Greater Prairie-Chicken's decline results from conversion of its native prairie habitat to agriculture. Some prairie-chickens have been restored to areas of Weld, Morgan, Logan, Washington, and Sedgwick Counties, but the sandhills of Yuma County remain the species' stronghold in Colorado.

Mary Taylor Gray's Colorado Birding Tip
### Dancing to the Pipes

Each spring, male Greater Prairie-Chickens perform an elaborate, stylized courtship dance to attract females. On an ancestral lek, or dancing ground, the males pirouette, erect specialized head feathers like small horns, and inflate orange air sacs on their throats like balloons. As the sacs deflate, the air squeezes out with a sighing wheeze. A lek full of strutting, displaying males sounds like a bagpipe band warming up. Colorado's Greater Prairie-Chicken leks are all on private land, mostly in Yuma County, but the Wray Museum, in partnership with the Division of Wildlife, offers guided viewing trips mid-April to mid-May. Call 970-332-5063.

*Tympanuchus pallidicinctus*

CORNELL LABORATORY OF ORNITHOLOGY

family: GROUSE and PTARMIGAN

**Field ID:** Mottled buff and brown plumage with black barring; paler undersides with brown barring; yellow comb over eyes; paler than the Greater Prairie-Chicken. *Male:* Red-orange neck sacs and ornamental neck feathers erected during courtship.
**Size:** 16 inches.

**Habitat:** Sand prairie characterized by tall grasses.

**Field Notes:** The Lesser Prairie-Chicken is quite similar in appearance to the Greater Prairie-Chicken, but the male lesser has red-orange air sacs in contrast to the yellow-orange sacs of the male greater. The lesser is slightly smaller, though this is of little help if the two are not side by side. Location is the best way to differentiate the two as the lesser was historically found only in southeastern Colorado and is now pretty much limited to Baca County on the Comanche National Grasslands around Campo. Due to loss of native habitat to agriculture and overgrazing, Lesser Prairie-Chickens are a threatened species in Colorado.

**Jan Feb Mar Apr May June July Aug Sept Oct Nov Dec**

*Tympanuchus phasianellus*

CORNELL LABORATORY OF ORNITHOLOGY

**Field ID:** Brownish plumage; scaled and spotted with black and buff. The white tail is wedge-shaped with protruding central feathers. *Male:* Yellow eye combs and purple neck sacs.
**Size:** 18 inches.

**Habitat:** Shrublands of oak, serviceberry, and sagebrush; wet meadows; aspen forests; riparian areas and agricultural land.

**Field Notes:** Like other grouse species, sharptails perform a courtship dance on a dancing ground, or lek. Biologists identify two subspecies, or different and distinct populations, of Sharp-tailed Grouse in Colorado: the Columbian sharptail, which inhabits northwestern Colorado, and the plains sharptail, formerly widespread across the northern two-thirds of eastern Colorado but now mainly limited to a small population in Douglas County. Like other ground-dwelling prairie birds, the sharptails' habitat has been largely converted to grazing and cropland. The Plains Sharp-tailed Grouse is endangered in Colorado.

*Meleagris gallopavo*

**Field ID:** Very large with iridescent bronze plumage. *Male:* Naked, blue head; red "wattles" (loose throat skin); feathery "beard" hanging from the breast. The male may be as much as four feet tall. *Female:* Duller and smaller than the male; lacks the colorful head, decorative wattles, and breast beard.
**Size:** *M:* 46 inches; *F:* 37 inches.

**Habitat:** Forests, mainly ponderosa pine with scrub oak and riparian areas; piñon-juniper woodlands; shrublands; wooded agricultural land.

**Field Notes:** The Wild Turkey's great size makes it a real head turner, whether moving along open ground or roosting high in the trees. Family groups of turkeys roost at night in mature trees, their large, dark shapes incongruous in the treetops. Turkeys are very intelligent and wary birds, drifting back into cover if they sense danger. The Anasazi and other native peoples of the Southwest domesticated turkeys, leaving evidence of them in ruins and cliff dwellings of southwestern Colorado. The native Merriam's subspecies is found through the foothills, canyons, and mesa country of southern Colorado. The Rio Grande subspecies was introduced as a game bird along waterways in eastern Colorado beginning in the early 1980s.

**Jan Feb Mar Apr May June July Aug Sept Oct Nov Dec**     *79*

*Colinus virginianus*

**Field ID:** Small head and plump, mottled, reddish-brown body with streaky sides. *Male:* Bold white throat and eye stripe. **Size:** 9¾ inches.

**Habitat:** Riparian areas adjacent to farm fields; sand prairie.

**Field Notes:** Bobwhites may have inhabited Colorado historically, but numbers were greatly boosted and their range expanded after introduction into the state as a game bird beginning in 1870. These charming little quail mill about, peeping in high-pitched tones. In spring, unmated males sound the familiar "bobwhite" call. Experts at the dramatic escape, a covey of bobwhites may explode practically from underfoot. Bobwhites live year-round in riparian areas of eastern Colorado, particularly along the South Platte and Arkansas River drainages.

*Callipepla squamata*

**Field ID:** Pale gray; scaly markings on breast and back; triangular, white-tipped head crest. **Size:** 10 inches.

**Habitat:** Sand prairie; farm and ranch lands; piñon-juniper woodlands; shrublands.

**Field Notes:** "Scalies" or "Cottontops," as they are affectionately nicknamed, are charming little quail whose white cotton-top crest gives them a look of perpetual surprise. Social birds, quail live together much of the year in coveys, which may number more than 100 birds. The covey breaks up for nesting. After the young leave the nest, family groups of adults and puff-ball chicks are often seen scurrying about beneath vegetation. Scaled Quail are common over much of the southern half of eastern Colorado.

*Callipepla gambelii*

**Field ID:** Plump and gray; reddish-brown sides streaked with white; characteristic head feather arching up from the forehead. *Male:* Distinctively marked with a reddish cap; black face and throat; white lines down the cheeks and across the forehead; black patch on the belly. *Female:* Pale gray face and throat; no dark patch on belly.
**Size:** 11 inches.

**Habitat:** Shrublands.

**Field Notes:** The Gambel's Quail looks like a tiny, avian sultan, the upright plume of its turban bobbing as it forages about on the ground in courtly fashion. The Gambel's, really a species of the desert Southwest, was introduced into Colorado beginning in 1885 and became established in far western Colorado in Garfield, Mesa, Montrose, and Delta Counties, where it is a year-round resident. Gambel's Quail require tall shrubs or trees for cover.

*Female*

*Geococcyx californianus*

family: CUCKOO

**Field ID:** Grayish-black, streaked and flecked with brown; white underparts; large head with shaggy crest; very long tail with white-tipped outer feathers; long heavy bill; long blue legs.
**Size:** 23 inches.

**Habitat:** Shrublands; piñon-juniper woodlands; grasslands.

**Field Notes:** While the cartoon roadrunner may seem like the lucky near-victim of Wile E. Coyote, the real-life roadrunner is nobody's fool. In addition to eating any insects and lizards it can catch, this plucky bird eats the fruits of cactus and catches scorpions, tarantulas, and snakes, including rattlesnakes. Legend credits the roadrunner with corralling snakes within a circle of cactus spines. Seeing a roadrunner in Colorado is a treat since they aren't common here, inhabiting the foothills and mesa country of southeastern Colorado.

# VIRGINIA RAIL

*Rallus limicola*

**Field ID:** Reddish-brown with black-streaked, olive-brown back; gray face; white chin; long, slightly down-curved, reddish bill. **Size:** 9½ inches.

**Habitat:** Marshy areas with cattails; wet meadows.

**Field Notes:** Rails are shy denizens of marshy areas, where they forage stealthily among the cattails and aquatic vegetation. Catching sight of a rail poking among the reeds at the edge of open water is a treat because at the slightest hint of danger, rails make themselves scarce, disappearing quietly back in among the vegetation. In spring, watchers are likely to hear the rail's chick-enlike *kik kik kik-kik-kik* calls, though they may never see the bird itself. Virginia Rails are found throughout eastern Colorado in summer, particularly along the South Platte and Arkansas River drainages, as well as in mountain parks and western valleys. A few remain through winter.

*Porzana carolina*

**Field ID:** Dark brown; streaked and mottled with white and black; grayish underneath; black face and throat; short yellow bill. **Size:** 8¾ inches.

**Habitat:** Marshy areas with cattails; wet meadows; irrigated hay meadows.

**Field Notes:** Like other rails, Soras are elusive, drifting out of sight among the cattails when danger threatens. Not as common in Colorado as Virginia Rails, their abundance is difficult to estimate due to their shy habits. A Sora is often heard rather than seen. In spring, its lonesome-sounding *pu-wee* call, rising on the "wee" portion, and its descending, chickenlike whinny, carry well across a marshland. The Sora's distribution in the state parallels that of the Virginia Rail—eastern Colorado, especially along river drainages, and mountain parks and valleys.

*Fulica americana*

**family: RAIL and GALLINULE**

**Field ID:** Black with a white, chickenlike bill and small head. The coot has large white spots on the covert feathers under its tail. **Size:** 15½ inches.

**Habitat:** Lakes, ponds, and reservoirs; marshes.

**Field Notes:** The coot, a black waterbird that resembles a duck but isn't one, is a common denizen of Colorado's ponds, lakes, and marshes. Its noisy gabbling, a combination of squawks, clucks and squeals, is responsible for its common name—mudhen. As coots swim, they pump their heads back and forth. Coots are found throughout the state in summer, their squawks and squabbles often audible when the birds themselves are hidden in the reeds. Some coots spend winter in eastern Colorado, particularly along the South Platte and Arkansas River drainages.

*Grus canadensis*

**Field ID:** Blue-gray with black wingtips; long sticklike legs; long neck and bill; naked red forehead.
**Size:** 41 inches.

**Habitat:** Wet meadows and farm fields; shallow water of ponds and reservoirs. Cranes nest in grassy, wet meadows of mountain parks.

**Field Notes:** The sight of dozens of Sandhill Cranes feeding in a stubble field seems like a scene from another epoch. Standing four feet tall, the cranes stride around on slender legs, occasionally leaping into the air as part of their courtship dance. The air fills with their raucous calls, which merge into a kind of trilling when many birds are calling. In March, north-bound migrating cranes gather in the San Luis Valley. Some nest in northwest Colorado and gather in large numbers around Hayden in Routt County in preparation for fall migration. A few **Whooping Cranes**, an endangered species, pass through Colorado during migration.

*Whooping Cranes*

*family: CRANE*

Mary Taylor Gray's Colorado Birding Tip
**Valley of Cranes**

The passage of up to 20,000 Sandhill Cranes through the San Luis Valley in mid-to-late March is a stunning sight not to be missed. The fields around Monte Vista and the wet meadows of the Monte Vista and Alamosa National Wildlife Refuges fill with the four-foot-tall birds, all calling loudly. Here and there birds bow and leap, fan their wings, and prance around as part of an elaborate courtship dance. Each year, in late March, the local chamber of commerce sponsors the Monte Vista Crane Festival (719-852-3552).

*Ceryle alcyon*

**Field ID:** Blue-gray with white breast and neck ring; gray-blue band across the chest. The head is large with a long heavy bill and a rough-cut crest. The female has a second band of chestnut across the belly. **Size:** 13 inches.

**Habitat:** Streams, rivers and canals; ponds, lakes, and reservoirs.

**Field Notes:** Perched on a twig overhanging the water, the kingfisher shows a unique profile, looking a bit as if it were put together by committee, with a head that seems too large for its body, a slanting flat-top crest with the look of a bad haircut, a short neck, heavy bill, and tiny feet. A kingfisher announces itself with a harsh, ratcheting cry as it flies along a stream course. Found year-round along streambeds of eastern Colorado, kingfishers are found throughout the state in summer.

*Pluvialis squatarola*

*Breeding plumage*

**Field ID:** *Breeding plumage:* Coal-black face, throat, and belly; white band from shoulder over crown to other shoulder; back and wings patterned in black and white. *Winter plumage:* A nondescript gray, with a faint eyebrow and black "armpits."
**Size:** 11½ inches.

family: PLOVER

**Habitat:** Shorelines and mudflats of lakes and reservoirs of eastern Colorado. Sometimes seen in fields and wet meadows.

**Field Notes:** The Black-bellied Plover is mainly a migrant through Colorado, its numbers highest in September and October. Like other shorebirds, it stops at the many open, mostly treeless reservoirs of eastern Colorado as it moves south during winter migration from its nesting grounds on the Arctic tundra. In breeding plumage, Black-bellied Plovers are handsome and distinctive, but they moult to drab gray after the breeding season, when they become harder to identify.

*Winter plumage*

*Charadrius melodus*

**Field ID:** Pale gray with snowy breast and face; black forehead band; black breast band. The breast band may be incomplete, especially in females. Legs are orange and the orange bill has a dark tip. The high piping call is distinctive.
**Size:** 7¼ inches.

**Habitat:** The sandy, bare shorelines of reservoirs in southeastern Colorado.

**Field Notes:** Piping Plovers are rare birds in Colorado, but eastern reservoirs provide valuable habitat for this threatened species. These little plovers have declined severely nationwide due to commercial development of their beach nesting habitat. Piping Plovers did not inhabit the native shortgrass prairie, but construction of irrigation reservoirs in eastern Colorado created the open beaches that plovers need for nesting. Numbers of Piping Plovers and nesting success vary greatly year to year due to water fluctuations that affect whether suitable beach habitat is available. **Snowy Plovers** are very similar to Piping Plovers but have white undersides and black bars on the shoulders rather than a neck ring.

*Snowy Plover*

Mary Taylor Gray's Colorado Birding Tip
**Threatened Plovers**

Piping Plovers nest on bare beaches and shorelines where their nests and young are very vulnerable to being trampled, driven over, or destroyed by dogs. The plovers have nested in recent years at Nee Noshe and Neegronda Reservoirs in Kiowa County, so visitors there, or at any other eastern plains reservoir offering potential plover habitat, need to be especially cautious to avoid harming this little sand-colored shorebird.

*Charadrius vociferus*

**Field ID:** Dark brown with snowy undersides; two distinctive black rings on throat and upper breast. In flight, the Killdeer's white and brown wings flash boldly. **Size:** 10½ inches.

**Habitat:** Shores of lakes and ponds; stream and river banks; grass-lands; gravel parking lots; farm fields.

**Field Notes:** The Killdeer is very common in Colorado and probably the most familiar shorebird to most people. Killdeer inhabit the edges of lakes, ponds, streams, parks, and open fields, sometimes even nesting in gravel parking lots. Their shrill shrieking call— *kill dee!*—sounds as they fly overhead or defend their territory on the ground. Killdeer are renowned for their broken-wing display. If an intruder, human or animal, comes too near its nest, the adult Killdeer hobbles along the ground dragging a wing and shrieking to draw the potential predator away from the nest.
**Semipalmated Plovers** look like small Killdeer but have only one black neck ring; at 7¼ inches they are much smaller.

*Semipalmated Plover*

family: PLOVER

*Charadrius montanus*

**Field ID:** Sandy-brown with paler underparts; white forehead bearing a black bar; large, dark eye with a black line between bill and corner of eye.
**Size:** 9 inches.

**Habitat:** Shortgrass prairie of eastern Colorado.

**Field Notes:** The Mountain Plover is a bird that defies expectations. Despite its name, this shorebird nests on the shortgrass prairie of eastern Colorado. Agricultural and urban development of the high plains has reduced native shortgrass prairie by as much as 90 percent, meaning loss of essential nesting habitat and severe population declines for the plover. This species is being considered for listing as a threatened species. The best place to look for Mountain Plovers is on the Pawnee National Grasslands in Weld County. Biologists estimate as many as 900 plovers may inhabit South Park. If you should spot plovers, be sure to watch from afar with binoculars to avoid stressing the birds or endangering the nest or young.

Mary Taylor Gray's Colorado Birding Tip
**Prairie Shorebirds**

Colorado's shortgrass prairie is a long way from any ocean, but two shorebirds have traditionally nested on our "prairie shores." Mountain Plovers and Long-billed Curlews were once widespread in summer on the central prairies of North America, but they have declined drastically with development of the Great Plains. The Pawnee National Grasslands in Weld County is a good place to spot Mountain Plovers, while the southern parcel of the Comanche National Grasslands in Baca County is probably best for Long-billed Curlews, though they may be seen during migration at reservoirs across much of eastern Colorado.

family: PLOVER

*Himantopus mexicanus*

**Field ID:** Black above with white underparts; long, straight black bill; long, pencil-thin pink or red legs; red eyes.
**Size:** 14 inches.

**Habitat:** Alkaline edges of lakes, ponds, reservoirs, and marshy shorelines.

**Field Notes:** The stilt is well named for there is no mistaking its long-legged form, needlelike bill, and formal black and white plumage. In flight, the stilt carries its legs trailing out behind like streamers. Despite its elegant appearance, once disturbed, the stilt becomes a screaming harpie, taking flight and circling with much shrill and persistent calling—*keek, keek, keek.* This incessant racket plus its black and white "suit" led to the stilt being nicknamed "lawyer bird." Watch for stilts in eastern Colorado at the edges of reservoirs, ponds, and flooded farm fields. A few also breed in the San Luis Valley and at the Arapaho National Wildlife Refuge near Walden in North Park.

Jan Feb Mar **Apr May June July Aug Sept** Oct Nov Dec      93

# AMERICAN AVOCET

*family: AVOCET and STILT*

*Recurvirostra americana*

**Field ID:** Bold black and white with rusty-orange neck and head; long legs; long needlelike bill that curves upward. The female's bill curves up more sharply than the male's. In winter the rusty head and neck fade to dull gray.
**Size:** 18 inches.

**Habitat:** Edges of treeless lakes, ponds, reservoirs, marshy shorelines, flooded fields, and temporary pools along country roads.

**Field Notes:** Avocets move on impossibly long, slender legs with the grace and bearing of a runway model. Their long, upcurved bills look as if they have been caught in a door. Avocets feed by striding through shallow water, sweeping the bill back and forth in the water to feel for prey. Avocets become shrill-voiced viragos once disturbed, screaming incessantly and dive-bombing intruders. Watch for them at shallow pools and lakes over much of the state, especially on the eastern plains and in North Park and the San Luis Valley.

Mary Taylor Gray's Colorado Birding Tip
**Shorebirds on the Eastern Plains**

Certainly arid, land-locked Colorado seems an odd place to find shore and wading birds, but the birds don't seem to know that. The barren shorelines of eastern Colorado's many irrigation reservoirs host thousands of shorebirds during spring and fall migration. Numbers vary greatly depending on water level. Good spots to check include Jackson and Union Reservoirs in Weld County; Barr Lake State Park in Adams County; the reservoirs of Queens State Wildlife Area (Nee So Pah, Nee Noshe, Neegronda, and Upper and Lower Queens) north of Lamar; and Horse Creek and Adobe Creek Reservoirs in Bent County.

*Tringa flavipes*

**Lesser Yellowlegs**                    **Greater Yellowlegs**

family: SANDPIPER

**Field ID:** The two species of yellowlegs are quite similar—long-legged wading birds with dark, streaked backs, necks, and heads; whitish underparts; yellow or orange legs. The **Greater Yellowlegs** is larger than the lesser and its bill is about one and one-half times the length of the head. The lesser's bill is about equal in length to its head. **Size:** *Lesser*—10½ inches; *Greater*—14 inches.

**Habitat:** Shores of lakes, ponds, and reservoirs; wet meadows.

**Field Notes:** The Lesser Yellowlegs strides around in shallow water, probing methodically for food. It is a very common Colorado visitor during fall migration—800 were counted on one day at Nee So Pah Reservoir in Kiowa County—and fairly common in spring, in eastern Colorado, western valleys, and the San Luis Valley. The Greater Yellowlegs passes through the same areas during its spring and fall migration. The **Solitary Sandpiper**, 8½ inches, is similar to the yellowlegs, though smaller. It has dark wings spotted with white, streaky brown head, and pale undersides. A bold, white eye ring and shorter legs help distinguish it from the Lesser Yellowlegs. Seen in Colorado only during migration, it is more common mid-July to late September.

**Solitary Sandpiper**

*Catoptrophorus semipalmatus*

**Field ID:** Large; gray with paler undersides; medium-length bill. The wings flash a bright white W when it flies.
**Size:** 15 inches.

**Habitat:** Grassy marshes; wet meadows; the edges of lakes, ponds, and reservoirs.

**Field Notes:** The Willet is not a particularly remarkable shorebird, until it takes flight. When the Willet unfolds its wings, the flash of bright white on black is startling. The bird's bright white tail adds to the surprising transformation, as does its shrill voice, screaming *pill-will-willet!* Willets are among a group of noisy shorebirds nicknamed "tattlers" for their telltale screams that announce the presence of intruders. In summer, some Willets nest in North Park. Otherwise watch for them from late April through mid-May on eastern reservoirs, with a few coming through again from August through mid-October.

*Actitis macularia*

**Field ID:** *Breeding plumage:* Brown back barred with black; snowy undersides dotted with telltale black spots. *Winter plumage:* The bird loses its spots and becomes quite similar to other sandpipers in winter plumage. **Size:** 7½ inches.

**Habitat:** Shorelines and shallow edges of lakes, ponds, reservoirs, streams, and wetland pools.

**Field Notes:** Tipping forward and back, bobbing up and down, the Spotted Sandpiper scurries busily along freshwater beaches and shores, earning the nicknames "teeter-bob," "tip-up," and "seesaw." Something of a maverick among its sandpiper cousins, the Spotted Sandpiper prefers freshwater habitats, swims and dives, sometimes perches on wires, and may nest high in the mountains along lakes and streams. It is found throughout the state, particularly on the Western Slope in summer. The **Upland Sandpiper,** a bird of inland sand-sage prairies, is larger than the spotted (12 inches), and is a barred, mottled brown with paler underparts. It has a small head, long neck, a tail that projects beyond the wingtips, and a short, yellow bill.

*Upland Sandpiper*

*Numenius americanus*

**Field ID:** Very large; mottled brown with cinnamon underparts; very long, down-curved bill. **Size:** 23 inches.

**Habitat:** Shortgrass prairie and farm fields of eastern Colorado, usually with standing water nearby. Along shorelines during migration.

**Field Notes:** With its unbelievably long beak, the Long-billed Curlew is a wondrous bird to see, and not easily confused with other species. In flight, its profile is quite dramatic, the curving bill held out like the nose cone of a fighter jet. While it may look as if it belongs on the seashore, curlews are prairie birds during nesting season. Once common throughout eastern Colorado, also nesting in North and Middle Parks, their numbers declined with development of native shortgrass prairie. They are now most common in the southeastern part of the state in Baca, Prowers, and Kiowa Counties.

*Limosa fedoa*

family: SANDPIPER

**Field ID:** Brown back mottled with black and cinnamon. Its long bill, which curves up very slightly, is distinctively colored pink with a dark tip. **Size:** 18 inches.

**Habitat:** Edges of eastern Colorado reservoirs and lakes.

**Field Notes:** Like other long-billed wading birds, the godwit is often seen in mixed flocks with smaller shorebirds whose varying bill lengths allow all to feed over the same ground, but at different depths, without competing with each other. In spring the flashy aerial courtship display of the godwit can be quite a sight as it carves figure eights in the air, its screaming *ratica-ratica-ratica* calls making it a hard bird to ignore. Marbled Godwits visit eastern Colorado during spring migration—mid-April to mid-May— and less commonly on their return migration south in August and September.

These sandpipers are similar in appearance and, though they vary in size, can be quite difficult to identify. They are generally seen in Colorado only during spring and fall migration, and then mainly on the reservoirs of eastern Colorado. Though they are in our state only briefly, these shorebirds may number in the hundreds or thousands when they do come through. They may show up occasionally in mountain parks and valleys. Migrating shorebirds are seen in Colorado in varying plumages—breeding, winter, or moulting between the two—which also complicates identification.

### SEMIPALMATED SANDPIPER *Calidris apusilla*

6¼ inches. This small sandpiper is pale brown and similar to the Least Sandpiper but has a longer, heavier bill. More common in late summer, from August to mid-September.

*Winter plumage*

### WESTERN SANDPIPER

*Calidris mauri*

6½ inches. A small sandpiper with a rusty back. May be quite abundant in late summer, from mid-August through September. It is seen more often in mountain parks than other sandpipers.

### LEAST SANDPIPER

*Calidris minutilla*

6 inches. This very small sandpiper has a streaked breast and head, yellow legs, and mottled back. More common in late summer and fall, from mid-August to early October. Hundreds may cluster at one location.

## WHITE-RUMPED SANDPIPER

*Calidris fuscicollis*

7½ inches. This streaked and mottled sandpiper is distinctive for its white upper tail coverts. It is seen almost exclusively in the spring, from mid-May to early June.

## BAIRD'S SANDPIPER

*Calidris bairdii*

7½ inches. This small sandpiper has a streaked, buffy breast and light-edged, brown plumage that gives it a scaly look. Abundant from early August to early October. Three thousand have been counted in one day at Jackson Reservoir in Morgan County.

## PECTORAL SANDPIPER

*Calidris melanotos*

8¾ inches. This medium-sized sandpiper is streaked and mottled with buffy-brown and black with paler undersides. More common in late summer and fall, from late August to late October.

## STILT SANDPIPER

*Calidris melanotos*

8½ inches. This medium-sized sandpiper is streaked and mottled with buffy-brown and black with paler undersides. More common in late summer and fall, from late August to late October. Two thousand have been counted in one day at Jackson Reservoir in Morgan County.

family: SANDPIPER

101

# LONG-BILLED DOWITCHER

*Limnodromus scolopaceus*

**Field ID:** Chunky body; relatively short legs; very long heavy bill. *Breeding plumage:* Cinnamon-red underparts with barring on breast and sides; wings mottled brownish-gray. In flight, watch for the barred tail and white rump. *Winter plumage:* Gray-brown back and lighter undersides. **Size:** 11½ inches.

**Habitat:** Shores of lakes and reservoirs during migration.

**Field Notes:** A migrating flock of Long-billed Dowitchers descending on the shore of an eastern reservoir is fun to watch, a collection of short-legged, plump-bodied, long-billed shore-birds all busily foraging. Flocks numbering nearly 1,000 birds have been sighted in eastern Colorado. The dowitcher's white rump is very noticeable in flight, and its high-pitched *keek, keek, keek* calls are distinctive. The Long-billed Dowitcher is a common fall migrant along the reservoirs of eastern Colorado, less common in spring. They also show up in mountain parks and Western Slope valleys.

*Gallinago gallinago*

family: SANDPIPER

**Field ID:** Mottled brown with lighter stripes and pale undersides. The head is boldly striped from front to back. This stocky, short-legged sandpiper has an extremely long bill and short tail, giving the snipe a distinctive flight profile. **Size:** 10½ inches.

**Habitat:** Streamsides; wet meadows; marshes; wet edges along country roads.

**Field Notes:** Many people doubt a bird called a snipe truly exists, thinking it only a mythical beast greenhorns are sent to capture with a gunny sack—the proverbial snipe hunt. Shy and secretive, snipes aren't easy to see except when performing their eerie, whistling courtship flight known as winnowing. Using its spread tail feathers as the violin, and the air as a bow, the snipe flies great loops and figures in the air, strumming out an airy whistling—*whoo, whoo, whoo*—that rises and falls in pitch as the bird carves the air. Snipes are found across the state in summer, with some spending winter at lower elevations in eastern Colorado, the San Luis Valley, and some western valleys.

*Phalaropus tricolor*

**Field ID:** *Breeding plumage:* Pale undersides; gray-brown back; cinnamon wash on the neck; broad dark streak that passes through the eye and down the side of the neck. *Winter plumage:* Gray above with white underparts. Phalaropes have a small head, long thin neck, and long straight bill. **Size:** 9¼ inches.

**Habitat:** Ponds; marshes; wet meadows; small lakes.

**Field Notes:** These long-necked shorebirds employ a distinctive feeding strategy. Phalaropes paddle jerkily about on shallow water, making sudden turns left or right and stabbing repeatedly with their bills. They often spin on the water, sometimes making 60 revolutions a minute. As they whirl they stir up the bottom, dislodging insects, larvae, and other food that is promptly gobbled up by the bird. Wilson's Phalaropes are common migrants through Colorado in both spring and fall, and quite a few spend summer on the ponds and wetlands of North Park and the San Luis Valley, as well as other western valleys and the eastern plains.

# RED-NECKED PHALAROPE

*Phalaropus lobatus*

*Female*

**Field ID:** *Breeding plumage:* Chestnut-red front and sides of the neck; white throat; dark back with bright buffy stripes. The male is duller than the female. *Winter plumage:* Both adults are a mottled gray and black with paler neck and undersides; black smudge across the eye. **Size:** 7¾ inches.

**Habitat:** Lakes and reservoirs, mainly of eastern Colorado during migration.

**Field Notes:** Red-necked Phalaropes pass through Colorado only briefly during migration—mid-May to early June and again late August through the end of September. But when they are here, there can be thousands of them in one flock. Two thousand individuals were counted in one day in mid-May on Prospect Reservoir in Weld County. In fall, the major staging areas for this species are Mono Lake, California, and Great Salt Lake, Utah, where more than half-a-million birds may gather.

*Winter plumage*

# FRANKLIN'S GULL

*Larus pipixcan*

family: GULL and TERN

**Field ID:** Dark gray wings with black and white bars on the wingtips; white neck and underparts; dramatic black hood covering the head. **Size:** 14½ inches.

**Habitat:** Reservoirs and lakes; farmland; plowed fields; urban areas.

**Field Notes:** Franklin's Gulls visit Colorado during migration, particularly in fall, though some remain in the state throughout summer. With their heads covered by a dark black hood, they look a bit like black-helmeted aviators as they wing by overhead. Construction of reservoirs in eastern Colorado provides habitat for these small gulls, and from August through mid-October they are quite abundant on the eastern plains. Franklin's Gulls are common enough throughout the Great Plains in summer that locals have nicknamed them "prairie doves."

# RING-BILLED GULL

*Larus delawarensis*

**Field ID:** White with black-tipped gray wings; yellow bill with a black ring near the tip. In winter, the white head is freckled with brown. Young birds are a mottled brown. **Size:** 17½ inches.

**Habitat:** Urban and suburban areas around dumps and garbage dumpsters; reservoirs; waterways; and farmland—particularly freshly plowed fields.

**Field Notes:** Familiar year-round residents in Colorado, Ring-billed Gulls may gather on rivers and lakes, and in flooded fields, where they stride about in no-nonsense fashion gobbling up insects and worms. Ring-billed Gulls also hang out in cities and suburbs at park ponds, restaurant parking lots, garbage dumps, or wherever they might scrounge up a meal. The ring-billed is our most common gull. It is fairly widespread across the state in summer, except for the high mountains and treeless areas of the eastern plains, concentrating along the South Platte and Arkansas River drainages in winter.

*Winter plumage*

# CALIFORNIA GULL

*Larus californicus*

**Field ID:** Dark gray and black wings with white wingtips. The head, neck, and undersides are snowy white; the bill yellow with black and red spots.
**Size:** 21 inches.

**Habitat:**
Reservoirs; water-ways; farmland—particularly freshly plowed fields. Nesting birds inhabit islands in the middle of lakes.

**Field Notes:** The California Gull looks much like the ring-billed but has a black and red spot on the lower bill instead of a black ring around the entire bill, and is quite a bit larger. Sometimes called a Mormon gull, the California Gull is renowned in Utah for saving the Mormon settlers' first crop by fortuitously arriving to devour a plague of locusts. California Gulls are abundant in Colorado during spring and fall migration. In summer look for them along the South Platte and Arkansas Rivers and in the mountains and western valleys.

Mary Taylor Gray's Colorado Birding Tip
### Don't Call them Seagulls

"Seagull" is the wrong term to use for gulls in Colorado since many of our birds are inland gulls that have never seen the ocean. Our most common gull, the ring-billed, is a familiar plains resident, where groups of them may be seen bobbing like a flotilla on a lake or waterway, scattered like white spots across a moist field, swarming garbage dumps, or hanging out in parking lots of fast-food restaurants, fighting over spilled french fries.

*family: GULL and TERN*

*Larus argentatus*

**Field ID:** *Summer plumage:* Snowy white with gray wings and black tail. *Winter plumage:* The white becomes freckled and streaked with brown. Winter is the most likely time to see these gulls in Colorado. **Size:** 25 inches.

**Habitat:** Reservoirs and lakes; open water.

**Field Notes:** Startlingly large if you should chance to see one up close, the Herring Gull has a wingspan of four and one-half feet. By mid-November, Herring Gulls arrive in our state in large numbers, mainly seeking open water along the South Platte and Arkansas River drainages. Some are seen every winter in the heart of Denver near the confluence of Cherry Creek and the South Platte River. Because of its size, the Herring Gull has no problem pirating food from other birds.

*Winter plumage*

*Sterna forsteri*

**family: GULL and TERN**

**Field ID:** White with pale gray mantle; deeply forked tail; orange bill with black tip. A black cap covers the head down to the eye line. The juvenile bird lacks the black cap and has a black patch around the eye. **Size:** 14½ inches.

**Habitat:** Lakes and reservoirs; nesting in cattail marshes along open water.

**Field Notes:** Terns are smaller, more slender, and more graceful than gulls, with tapered, pointed wings and deeply forked tails, leading to a common nickname, "sea swallow." With their sleek wings, they swoop and swerve, cutting and slicing the air in acrobatic flight. Terns typically hunt by flying over open water, heads bent downward as they scan the water for fish. Plunge-diving from the air, they hit the water dramatically as they snatch at prey. Forster's Terns are fairly common across eastern Colorado during spring and fall, spending summer mainly along the South Platte, Arkansas, and Rio Grande River drainages, as well as in the San Luis Valley and North Park.

*Sterna antillarum*

**Field ID:** Gray with black cap and nape; white throat, forehead, and underparts; short, deeply forked tail. In flight watch for black wingtips. **Size:** 9 inches.

**Habitat:** Reservoirs and lakes.

**Field Notes:** The smallest of North American terns, the Least Tern is listed both federally and in Colorado as an endangered species, suffering the same habitat losses as Piping Plovers. In the nineteenth century, Least Terns were slaughtered by the hundreds of thousands for the millinery trade, their wings and entire skins used to decorate women's hats. Least Terns were very rare on the native prairie, but reservoirs built for irrigation on the eastern plains created habitat for them. They nest on bare, sandy shores of exposed islands and sandbars. Nesting success varies year to year depending on fluctuating water levels. Least Terns have nested at Adobe Creek and Nee Noshe Reservoirs in Kiowa County, and Horse Creek Reservoir in Otero County. Caution: Be very careful not to disturb the birds or their nests when visiting potential nesting sites.

Jan Feb Mar Apr May **June July Aug Sept** Oct Nov Dec    *111*

*Chlidonias niger*

family: GULL and TERN

**Field ID:** Dark-charcoal body and wings; appearing all black in most light. The undersides of the wings are pale gray and there is white under the tail, which is short and slightly forked.
**Size:** 9¾ inches.

**Habitat:** Reservoirs and lakes; cattail marshes along open water.

**Field Notes:** Small, sleek aerialists, Black Terns sometimes fly erratically, abruptly shifting direction after spotting prey. In flight, they look strongly two-toned—dark above, their paler undersides appearing white. They are particularly abundant during spring migration, roughly from early May into June. Watch for them in eastern Colorado and hunting above ponds in mountain parks, including the Arapaho National Wildlife Refuge near Walden in North Park. In summer some nest along the South Platte and Arkansas Rivers, in mountain parks, and in the San Luis Valley. Black Terns have been declining throughout their range due to pesticides, human disturbance, and loss of marshland nesting habitat.

*Columba livia*

family: DOVE and PIGEON

**Field ID:** Iridescent gray, green, and blue with purple highlights; white rump; black wing bars. The head and neck are darker than the body. Plumage is highly variable. Some Rock Doves can be mottled, white, or spotted. **Size:** 12½ inches.

**Habitat:** Cities and suburbs; farmland; cliffs and canyons; rocky areas near open country.

**Field Notes:** Rock Dove is the official common name of a very familiar bird, the city pigeon. They seem to be everywhere—under bridges and overpasses, on neighborhood power lines, on window ledges of tall buildings. Like unwelcome relatives, they move into towns and cities and make themselves at home. But Rock Doves also live in the wild, in canyons and rocky areas. Rock Doves vary greatly in their plumage, the result of thousands of years of domestication. They were the first bird to be domesticated, originally for food, though later they were used as carrier and homing pigeons. Not native to North America, Rock Doves were first brought to Nova Scotia by the French in 1606 and spread across the continent from escaped and released birds.

**Jan Feb Mar Apr May June July Aug Sept Oct Nov Dec**    *113*

*Columba fasciata*

*family: DOVE and PIGEON*

**Field ID:** Grayish-brown with iridescent-purple breast and head; slate blue wings; broad gray band on tail; yellow legs; yellow bill with dark tip. The nape of the neck is greenish with a white band. **Size:** 14½ inches.

**Habitat:** Ponderosa pine forests; oakbrush; riparian zones; agricultural areas with open woodlands or tree stands.

**Field Notes:** The Band-tailed Pigeon looks very similar to its cousin, the Rock Dove or city pigeon. But instead of the Rock Dove's great variation in plumage, a flock of Band-tailed Pigeons all look alike. They often roost in the tops of trees and, when not nesting, gather in large flocks. The male takes up a perch in a tree and coos a deep, owl-like call—*whoo-hoo-hoo*. Band-tailed Pigeons arrive in Colorado in mid-April, returning to wintering grounds in Mexico and Central America by mid-October. They are most common in the foothills and low-elevation mountains of southern Colorado.

*Zenaida macroura*

family: DOVE and PIGEON

**Field ID:** Grayish-green with a pinkish cast; small head; black spots on the wings; iridescent green-purple sheen on the neck. The long, pointed tail is shaped like a spade, with white edges very noticeable in flight. **Size:** 12 inches.

**Habitat:** Open wooded habitats in lowlands and foothills, including city parks, greenbelts, and backyards; agricultural lands; riparian zones; shrublands; ponderosa pine forests; occasionally higher altitude aspen and coniferous forests.

**Field Notes:** The gentle Mourning Dove is a familiar friend, whether striding about the ground, its small head bobbing back and forth with each step, or perched in yards, parks, golf courses, or practically anywhere we turn. In flight the Mourning Dove's rounded head, long tail, and stubby wings form a stylized cross. The soft, sad cooing that gives the dove its name provides sweet music, punctuated by the whistling of its wing feathers as it flies up to roost. Mourning Doves mate for life, the two sitting side by side as the male coos softly and the female quietly answers.

Jan Feb Mar Apr **May June July Aug Sept** Oct Nov Dec    *115*

# BARN OWL

*Tyto alba*

**Field ID:** Slim-bodied with pearly-white plumage marked by tan streaking. The face is distinctively heart shaped.
**Size:** 16 inches.

**Habitat:** Agricultural land; grasslands; riparian areas; cliffs; earthen banks; barns and old buildings.

**Field Notes:** These beautiful, pale golden birds adapt well to life around humans, taking up residence in barns, silos, church steeples, and other old buildings. But due to their nocturnal habits, they are rarely seen. Barn Owls are birds of open country, found more often in eastern Colorado, though also in western valleys. They mainly visit Colorado from spring through fall. Biologists are concerned this owl is declining throughout its range.

Mary Taylor Gray's Colorado Birding Tip
**Dueting with Owls**

You don't always have to see a bird to enjoy its presence. If you hear an owl at night as you're sitting around the campfire, try echoing back its calls and see if you can't strike up a duet. Two common Colorado owls, the great horned and the western screech, often respond readily to answering hoots. The great horned's call is a classic, hollow *hoo hoo-hoo hoooo*, while the Western Screech-Owl sounds a hooting whinny that picks up in tempo but remains on one pitch.

*Otus flammeolus*

**Field ID:** Mottled gray or reddish-brown; small feathery "horns" or ear tufts; eyes dark instead of yellow. **Size:** 6¾ inches.

**Habitat:** Mature and old-growth ponderosa pine forests; aspen groves; piñon-juniper woodlands.

**Field Notes:** This tiny, secretive owl, the length of a sparrow, is not likely to be seen, even though it is probably more numerous than previously thought. On summer nights near mountain pine forests, listen for its mellow call, a hollow *boop*. "Flammulated," meaning flame-shaped, refers to the bird's mottled plumage. This excellent camouflage allows the bird to hide in plain sight, another reason watchers are very lucky to spot one. Flammulated Owls are summer visitors to pine forests of the western half of Colorado.

Jan Feb **Mar Apr May June July Aug Sept Oct** Nov Dec

# WESTERN SCREECH-OWL

*Otus kennicottii*

**Field ID:** Gray with highly mottled, camouflaged plumage; paler below; yellow eyes; short "horns" or ear tufts.
**Size:** 8½ inches.

**Habitat:** Riparian woodlands; urban open space; piñon-juniper forests.

**Field Notes:** With its feathery horns, this small owl looks a bit like a Great Horned Owl in miniature. The screech-owl is well camouflaged and hard to see, but listen for its voice, a whinny of *hoo-hoo-hoo* calls, speeding up, all on one note. Western Screech-Owls are concentrated in the southeast part of the state, where they live year-round. They also are found along wooded river drainages of the Western Slope and occasionally in city parks and urban open space. The **Eastern Screech-Owl,** very similar to the western, inhabits northeastern Colorado. Its call is a falling whinny.

*Eastern Screech-Owl*

family: TYPICAL OWL

**Jan Feb Mar Apr May June July Aug Sept Oct Nov Dec**

*Bubo virginianus*

**Field ID:** Brown plumage with a great deal of black barring; big yellow eyes; white throat; two feathery "horns" on the head. Gold feathery disks frame the face. **Size:** 22 inches.

**Habitat:** Riparian woodlands, especially on the edge of open country; agricultural land; urban and suburban open space and landscaping; and pine forests.

**Field Notes:** The great horned is the most common and widespread owl in Colorado, found throughout the state year-round, though mainly at lower elevations. Its large, cylindrical body can often be spotted during the day when the bird is roosting in trees, usually close to the trunk. Great Horned Owls are especially visible in winter, when the leaves are off the trees. Listen for the classic *hoo hoo-hoo hoooo* call of this hoot owl.

**Jan Feb Mar Apr May June July Aug Sept Oct Nov Dec**

# BURROWING OWL

*Athene cunicularia*

family: TYPICAL OWL

**Field ID:**
Brown plumage flecked and streaked with white; dark collar and white eyebrows. It has a round head, long legs, and very yellow eyes.
**Size:** 9½ inches.

**Habitat:** Prairie dog towns and prairie grasslands.

**Field Notes:** Burrowing Owls are about the same height and shape of a prairie dog, with a rounded head. They are usually seen perched on a burrow mound or low fence post or flying within a prairie dog town. This charming, ground-dwelling owl, so dependent upon shortgrass prairie habitat, has declined significantly with the loss of its habitat and its host species, the black-tailed prairie dog. Burrowing Owls, under consideration for listing as a threatened species, are summer visitors mainly to eastern Colorado.

Mary Taylor Gray's Colorado Birding Tip
**Little Ground Owls of the Prairie**

Have you ever driven by a prairie dog town in eastern Colorado when you thought you saw one of the prairie dogs jump in the air and fly off? That flying 'dog was a Burrowing Owl, a small owl that nests in prairie dog burrows. At a quick glance, Burrowing Owls are about the height and shape of a prairie dog, and often perch atop the burrow mounds. Scan an active 'dog town and you may discover several owls among the rodents. Populations of these fascinating ground-dwelling owls have declined severely due to the elimination of prairie dog towns in the face of agricultural and residential development.

*Asio otus*

**Field ID:** Gray-brown and rust with black streaking; close-set ear tufts; rust-colored facial disks. The long feathers of the wings extend beyond the tail of the perched bird. **Size:** 15 inches.

**Habitat:** Riparian areas; urban and suburban woodlands; Douglas-fir forests; occasionally aspen, piñon-juniper, and other mountain woodlands. Prefers dense forests and undergrowth rather than open woodlands.

**Field Notes:** This shy woodland owl has ear tufts like a great horned, but is quite a bit smaller and slighter and its plumage is streaked (vertical pattern) rather than barred (horizontal pattern) as is the great horned's. When distressed, the long-eared can draw itself up to appear very long and slender. Its camouflage plumage blends perfectly into the dabbled woodland habitat it prefers. The long-eared calls in a series of slow hoots as well as a ghostly *woo*. It is found year-round throughout the state, though more likely at lower elevations.

family: TYPICAL OWL

# SHORT-EARED OWL

*Asio flammeus*

**Field ID:** Rusty-brown back with buff mottling; paler under-sides streaked with brown. Yellow eyes are circled with dark feathers resembling eyeglasses. A ruff surrounds the face, giving a very round-faced appearance. Tiny, close-set "horns" are hard to see.
**Size:** 15 inches.

**Habitat:** Shortgrass prairie; open fields; ranch land; marshes.

**Field Notes:** The Short-eared Owl often begins its hunting in very late afternoon, making it one of the more readily seen owls. It hunts close above the ground over grasslands and marshes, its wing-beats fluttering and mothlike, and it often pauses and hovers above likely prey. Short-eared Owls, mainly winter visitors, are not common in Colorado and their numbers are declining. Some birds live year-round in eastern Colorado and in the San Luis Valley.

*Aegolius acadicus*

family: TYPICAL OWL

**Field ID:** Dark gray-brown with paler undersides heavily streaked with brown. This songbird-sized owl has a large round head with big, yellow eyes set in large facial disks. **Size:** 8 inches.

**Habitat:** Mountain pine and fir forests; piñon-juniper woodlands.

**Field Notes:** As a group, owls are always interesting birds, their large, forward-facing eyes rather humanlike. The tiny Saw-whet Owl is no exception, looking like a cartoon professor with its bulging head and huge eyes. Because of its shy nature and nocturnal habits, the saw-whet is not likely to be seen, but its voice, a high-pitched piping or whistling, may be heard in mountain forests. Saw-whet Owls are found in foothills and lower mountains year-round.

Jan Feb Mar Apr May June July Aug Sept Oct Nov Dec

# COMMON NIGHTHAWK

*Chordeiles minor*

family: NIGHTJAR

**Field ID:** Brownish-black mottled with white. The nighthawk has a blunt, rounded head; long, notched tail; and long, pointed, tapering wings with broad, white bars between the wrists and wingtips. **Size:** 9½ inches.

**Habitat:** Grasslands; farm and ranch land; shrublands; riparian woodlands; towns and cities; ponderosa pine; and piñon-juniper forests.

**Field Notes:** You will probably only see nighthawks in flight, usually in the evening or morning, but possibly anytime when it is cloudy. At times the sky may be filled with their crescent shapes, soaring at varying heights. Flying nighthawks call to each other with a nasal *peent.* Watch for the courtship flight, known as booming. A high-flying nighthawk suddenly plummets downward, then pulls up in a J-pattern and sounds a loud, airy *schoomp* as air rushes through the primary (fingertip) wing feathers. Nighthawks visit Colorado late spring through early fall.

*Phalaenoptilus nuttallii*

**Field ID:** Round-headed; short-tailed; very well camouflaged with plumage speckled brown, gray, and white; white collar; very large eyes. **Size:** 7¾ inches.

**Habitat:** Foothills; mesas; piñon-juniper and lower elevation ponderosa pine forests; riparian areas; grasslands adjacent to these habitats.

**Field Notes:** In the summer night, the eerie *poo-oo-wee* call of the poorwill is a familiar sound in the foothills and mesas of Colorado. Cousins to nighthawks, poorwills come out to hunt later in the evening. They flutter around like giant moths, snapping up insects in their wide mouths, or spring from the ground to grab a passing meal, then settle back to the same spot. Any sighting of a poorwill will likely be a quick glimpse of a low-flying bird or one perched on the highway, its eyes glowing pink in the shine of headlights. Poorwills are summer visitors to Colorado, from Eastern Slope foothills across the western half of the state.

# BLACK SWIFT

*Cypseloides niger*

B. MOOSE PETERSON

family: SWIFT

**Field ID:** All black with long, slender, pointed wings; fairly long notched tail. **Size:** 7¼ inches.

**Habitat:** Mountain cliffs and waterfalls, and adjacent forests and open country.

**Field Notes:** You will likely only see this, or any, swift in flight, as this group of birds lives on the wing, feeding, courting, and even mating in the air. Black Swifts are known for their habit of nesting behind waterfalls. They are birds of rugged cliff country, though they range across mountain forests and meadows hunting insects. Black Swifts are found very locally in Colorado and only in summer. Their winter grounds are unknown.

---

Mary Taylor Gray's Colorado Birding Tip
### Black Swifts

Like black boomerangs with minds of their own, Black Swifts dive, wheel, and fly on scimitar-shaped wings. Don't expect to see these incomparable aerialists, which like to nest behind mountain waterfalls, anywhere but in the air. Best places to look for them are at Hanging Lakes above I-70 in Glenwood Canyon and in Box Canyon Falls near Ouray.

---

*Chaetura pelagica*

CORNELL LABORATORY OF ORNITHOLOGY

**Field ID:** Dark grayish-brown with paler throat and chest; very long, slender, pointed wings. **Size:** 5¼ inches.

**Habitat:** Cities, towns, suburbs, and adjacent riparian areas.

**Field Notes:** The Chimney Swift's name is well earned, as these high-flying birds prefer to nest in crevices and chimneys of buildings. The Chimney Swift, a relatively new arrival in Colorado, is expanding its range westward as human habitation creates appropriate habitat across the Great Plains. Chimney Swifts are found in eastern Colorado from spring through fall, particularly along the South Platte and Arkansas River basins. Watch for them in evening, swirling above their roost sites or hunting the skies over cities and towns.

Jan Feb Mar Apr May **June July Aug** Sept Oct Nov Dec

# WHITE-THROATED SWIFT

*Aeronautes saxatalis*

**Field ID:** Black with white throat; broad, white stripe down breast and belly. White patches along the flanks contrast with dark patches under the long, slender wings. **Size:** 6½ inches.

**Habitat:** Cliffs and canyons.

**Field Notes:** On the wing, swifts are aerial poetry. Their long, slender wings cut the air like knives, carrying them swooping between canyon walls like stunt jets. In the airspace above a steep-walled canyon, the swifts flash back and forth, arcing and diving with incredible speed and grace. Their charming calls echo off the rocks in a laughing chatter. White-throated Swifts are summer visitors to Colorado in low-elevation cliff and canyon regions over the western part of the state.

*Progne subis*

**Field ID:** *Male:* Dark purple with black wings and tail. *Female:* Dull purple back; pale undersides; black wings and tail.
**Size:** 8 inches.

**Habitat:** Aspen forests adjacent to mountain parks with water; riparian areas; reservoirs; open land.

**Field Notes:** Purple Martins are common in the eastern United States where bird-lovers put up large condominium-style birdhouses for these communal nesting birds. But in Colorado, Purple Martins spend summer in only a few locations in lower elevation Western Slope mountains, particularly in northern parts of Mesa, Delta, and Gunnison Counties. Also look for them near some ponds below the east side of McClure Pass near Carbondale. Western populations of Purple Martins rarely nest in colonies.

# TREE SWALLOW

*Tachycineta bicolor*

family: SWALLOW

**Field ID:** Iridescent, almost metallic, blue back; white under-parts; round head; slightly forked tail. **Size:** 5¾ inches.

**Habitat:** Mountain aspen and coniferous forests; lowland riparian woodlands.

**Field Notes:** Tree Swallows usually nest in tree cavities near water, particularly in mountain aspen forests. They compete with other cavity nesters for homes but will use nest boxes, which have helped increase their numbers. Tree Swallows nest throughout the western mountains in summer, with occasional nesting on the eastern plains. They are found statewide during migration.

*Tachycineta thalassina*

### Field ID:

Iridescent green with purple shading; bright white underparts extending onto the cheeks and up on either side of the rump. The female is duller and appears more brownish than the male. **Size:** 5¼ inches.

**Habitat:** Cliffs and canyons and adjacent aspen and coniferous forests; mountain stream courses; valleys near water.

### Field Notes:

Milling in the air space above a canyon or flying over open country in pursuit of insects, Violet-green Swallows put on an amazing show of aerobatics—darting, swooping, and wheeling on a dime. You may need to look closely to differentiate them from White-throated Swifts, which share their cliff habitat, and from Tree Swallows, which also nest in the high country. The swift has a pattern of black and white on its underside, the Tree Swallow is cleanly colored dark on its back and white underneath, and the Violet-green Swallow is white underneath with white patches spreading up onto the lower back. Watch for violet-greens in summer and during migration over the western half of the state.

family: SWALLOW

*Stelgidopteryx serripennis*

**Field ID:** Brown with grayish breast, chin, and sides; whitish belly. **Size:** 5½ inches.

**Habitat:** Riparian areas; sandy banks along stream and river courses; farm and ranch land.

**Field Notes:** Swallows can be a little tricky to identify when they are milling in great crowds, wheeling and diving at breakneck speeds. The roughwing is perhaps the least distinctive of Colorado swallows, with no identifying colors, patterns, or tail shape. It nests in sandy banks along streams and bluffs. Watch for slower, deeper wing-beats to help differentiate it from the Bank Swallow. Look for roughwings in Colorado in summer on the eastern plains and in western valleys.

# BANK SWALLOW

*Riparia riparia*

**Field ID:** Dark brown with white throat and underparts; distinctive brown neck collar. White also extends behind the ears. **Size:** 5¼ inches.

**Habitat:** Sandbanks along waterways; bluffs; adjacent farm and ranch land.

**Field Notes:** A steep, sandy riverbank dotted with numerous holes is a good indicator of the colony-nesting Bank Swallow. The swallow's nest burrow can be differentiated from a kingfisher's by the lack of grooves in the floor of the entrance. Kingfishers typically leave such telltale grooves by dragging their feet upon entering. The Bank Swallow's wing-beats are rapid and shallow, unlike those of the Rough-winged Swallow. Bank Swallows are found in Colorado in summer, widespread across the east, and in western parks and valleys.

Jan Feb Mar Apr **May June July Aug Sept** Oct Nov Dec

# CLIFF SWALLOW

*Petrochelidon pyrrhonata*

**Field ID:** Blue-black with pale belly; gray sides; rusty-red face and rump; white crescent on the forehead. The tail is square, not forked. **Size:** 5½ inches.

**Habitat:** Cliffs and riverbanks; buildings and dams; under bridges; always near water.

**Field Notes:** Cliff Swallows are the clockwork birds that legend says faithfully return to the Mission San Juan Capistrano in southern California every March 19. Though Cliff Swallows do return each spring to the mission, the date varies slightly, depending on weather and seasonal conditions. Cliff Swallows also show up faithfully in Colorado each spring, nesting pretty much statewide. They may build huge colonies of mud nests beneath a bridge or overhang.

# BARN SWALLOW

*Hirundo rustica*

**Field ID:** Glossy blue-black on back and wings; brick-red breast becoming paler below. The long tail is deeply forked; white spots sometimes visible. **Size:** 6¾ inches.

**Habitat:** Farm and ranch land; towns, cities and suburbs; riparian areas; wetlands.

**Field Notes:** The Barn Swallow is easily differentiated from all other Colorado swallows, even in a crowd, by its deeply forked "swallow tail." It is also handsomely colored in deep blue and brick red. Barn Swallows adapt well to life around humans and often build their nests beneath the eaves of buildings and houses. They are found over most of Colorado in summer.

> Mary Taylor Gray's Colorado Birding Tip
> ### Swallows: Masters of the Air
>
> Swallows are masters of the aerial maneuver, swooping, diving, cutting, and wheeling on the wing, their laughing and chattering calls enlivening Colorado's air spaces. In the mountains watch for Tree and Violet-green Swallows; in rocky, canyon country look for Violet-green and Cliff Swallows; near water watch for Cliff, Bank, Barn, and Rough-winged Swallows. Both Barn and Cliff Swallows adapt well to life around humans and often build their nests under bridges and the eaves of buildings and houses.

Jan Feb Mar **Apr May June July Aug Sept Oct** Nov Dec

# BLACK-CHINNED HUMMINGBIRD

*Archilochus alexandri*

family: HUMMINGBIRD

**Field ID:** *Male:* Iridescent green; black throat edged by white collar below it. A purple patch on the lower throat flashes in the light. *Female:* Green with white underparts. **Size:** 3¾ inches.

**Habitat:** Piñon-juniper woodlands; oakbrush shrublands; riparian areas of foothills and lowlands; urban areas.

**Field Notes:** Male hummingbirds perform elaborate courtship flights in spring, each species with a characteristic flight pattern. The black-chin flies back and forth like a buzzing pendulum in front of the object of his interest, winging up 15 feet in the air, then zooming down and up again in an arc, his wings whirring like a very loud bee. Black-chins nest in summer, mainly in valleys and foothills of western and southern Colorado, occasionally showing up at feeders in other parts of the state.

*Female*

Jan Feb Mar Apr **May June July Aug Sept** Oct Nov Dec

# CALLIOPE HUMMINGBIRD

*Stellula calliope*

**Field ID:** *Male:* Emerald-green back and wings; pale undersides with purple streaking on the pale throat. Some of the purple feathers project beyond the throat like whiskers. *Female:* Green above and pale below; buffy wash across the breast and under the wings. **Size:** 3¼ inches.

**Habitat:** Ponderosa pine forests; mountain meadows; foothills; riparian woodlands; near hummingbird feeders.

**Field Notes:** In a family of tiny birds, the calliope is the tiniest, measuring only 2¾ to 3½ inches long, including the bill. Calliope Hummingbirds are in fact the smallest birds in the United States, weighing only one-tenth of an ounce. Calliopes pass through Colorado during their southerly migration in late July and August, showing up at feeders.

*Selasphorus platycercus*

**Field ID:** *Male:* Iridescent-green back and wings; whitish undersides. The throat flashes magenta-red in the light. *Female:* Iridescent green with buffy, faintly streaked undersides. **Size:** 4 inches.

**Habitat:** Mountain meadows; riparian areas; forests, including ponderosa pine, Douglas-fir, aspen, and piñon-juniper; willow thickets.

family: HUMMINGBIRD

*Female*

**Field Notes:** The broadtail is the classic hummingbird of the Colorado high country, arriving in late April and early May, then departing the state by late September. Broadtails come readily to feeders. They will also feed at the wells drilled in bark by sapsuckers. During spring and fall migration, broadtails show up at lower elevations including riparian areas and urban landscaping on the eastern plains.

Mary Taylor Gray's Colorado Birding Tip
**Summer's Hummers**

A shrill, familiar buzz announces one of the headliners of summer in the Colorado Rockies, the Broad-tailed Hummingbird. These iridescent-green "flower kissers" visit wildflower meadows, willow thickets, and hummingbird feeders in search of sugary nectar. While all hummingbirds make a whirring sound with their wings, only the male broadtail produces that distinctive buzz-bomb whine. Special tapered feathers at the tips of the wings create slots through which wind whistles when the bird flies, making that familiar trilling.

*Selasphorus rufus*

**Field ID:** *Male:* Iridescent copper with iridescent-red throat and white collar. *Female:* Iridescent-green back; coppery sides and tail; white undersides; white, speckled throat. **Size:** 3¾ inches.

**Habitat:** Coniferous and riparian forests of foothills and mountains; mountain meadows; suburban areas with feeders.

**Field Notes:** The Rufous Hummingbird passes through Colorado's mountains and foothills in July and August, heading to its Central American wintering range from nesting grounds in the Northwest. The rufous's Colorado stay is brief, but when this gleaming little bird is in town, you know it. Colored a glowing copper, the tiny male rufous is among the most aggressive of humming-birds, taking over a feeder and fiercely driving away competitors, including the larger but more docile broadtail.

*Female*

Mary Taylor Gray's Colorado Birding Tip
**The Rufous Invasion**

Like the bad boys of summer, Rufous Hummingbirds arrive in Colorado with a show of bravado, ready to take over the neighborhood bars and bully the locals. Once a rufous discovers a feeder, it moves in, drinking its fill then taking up a guard post nearby to keep away trespassers. Extremely aggressive, these copper-colored sprites will dive-bomb and drive off Broad-tailed Hummingbirds that may have used a feeder all summer. Watch for rufous hummers from mid-July to mid-September.

*Melanerpes lewis*

**Field ID:** Dark green back that appears black in dull light; pink belly; ruby face; white collar.
**Size:** 10¾ inches.

**Habitat:** Riparian woodlands; wooded areas of farm and ranch land; suburban areas; piñon-juniper woodlands.

**Field Notes:** In flight this handsome woodpecker is often mistaken for a crow. In the right light, it glows a deep green with a ruby-

red face and pinkish breast. Named for Meriwether Lewis of the Lewis and Clark Expedition, the Lewis's is an interesting member of the woodpecker family. It swoops out like a flycatcher to snag insects in flight and caches nuts and acorns in tree crevices. It is a year-round inhabitant of wooded areas of southern Colorado and occasionally shows up elsewhere in the state.

*family:* WOODPECKER

Mary Taylor Gray's Colorado Birding Tip
**The Un-Woodpecker Woodpecker**

The riparian woodlands and wooded farmland of southern Colorado are home to the Lewis's Woodpecker, a handsome bird that seems not to have read the "How to Be a Woodpecker" handbook. It flies with even wing-beats, like a crow, not the bursts and glides of other woodpeckers. It doesn't peck into tree bark for food but instead sallies out from a perch to hawk insects in flight like a flycatcher, glean insects from leaves like a warbler, and break nuts into pieces and wedge them in bark crevices like a nuthatch. It is also more likely to be seen perched atop a fence post than clinging to the side of a tree like any self-respecting woodpecker should.

*Melanerpes erythrocephalus*

**Field ID:** Body and wings patterned in blocks of black and white; red head and neck. **Size:** 9¼ inches.

**Habitat:** Lowland riparian woodlands; wooded areas of farm and ranch land.

**Field Notes:** Looking as if it has been dipped headfirst to the shoulders in red paint, this strikingly patterned bird is the only woodpecker whose head is all red. The body is colored in bold blocks of black and white. In flight, the white rump and white patches on the inner, trailing edges of the wings flash in dramatic contrast to the black plumage. In summer look for Red-headed Woodpeckers in wooded areas of eastern Colorado. The **Red-bellied Woodpecker** is sometimes found on the eastern plains, mainly in the northeast corner of the state. Its back is barred in black and white with a red crown and nape.

family: WOODPECKER

*Red-bellied Woodpecker*

*Sphyrapicus nuchalis*

**Field ID:** Black and white back; red forehead, throat, and nape; wide black and white stripes on the side of the head. Brownish juvenile.
**Size:** 8½ inches.

### Habitat:

Mountain aspen forests and coniferous forests; riparian areas during migration.

### Field Notes:

Seeking sap and soft, inner bark, sapsuckers drill orderly rows of holes in live trees, often making a checkerboard pattern

described as looking like apartment house windows. The Red-naped Sapsucker is common in the Colorado mountains. The **Williamson's Sapsucker** is sometimes found in foothills and lower mountains along the Eastern Slope and in southwestern Colorado. The male has a black back; red throat; white rump and wing patches. The female has a brown head and brown and white barred back.

*Williamson's Sapsucker*

Jan Feb Mar Apr **May June July Aug Sept** Oct Nov Dec

*Picoides pubescens*

*Female*

**Field ID:** Checkered black and white wings; white back and undersides; black crown; broad black and white bars across the face. Males have a red spot on the back of the head and nape.
**Size:** 6¾ inches.

**Habitat:** Riparian areas; cities, towns and suburbs with mature trees; mountain coniferous and aspen forests.

**Field Notes:** With a bill that looks less adapted for drilling wood than for eating seeds, the downy is the smallest American woodpecker. Adapting to life around humans, downies are decorous neighbors, taking up residence in city and suburban trees, checking out feeders, and going about their chores unperturbed by humans. Surprise a downy poised on the side of a tree and it may not fly off but instead hop around the trunk and peer back from the far side. Its whinnying call, dropping rapidly in pitch, is a familiar sound in both backyards and woodlands.

**Jan Feb Mar Apr May June July Aug Sept Oct Nov Dec**    *143*

*Picoides villosus*

**Field ID:** White back and undersides; black wings checkered with white; black crown; broad black and white bars across the face. Males have a red spot on the back of the head and nape.
**Size:** 9¼ inches.

**Habitat:** Mountain coniferous and aspen forests; lowland riparian areas; piñon-juniper woodlands; urban and suburban landscaping.

**Field Notes:** Though quite similar in appearance to the Downy Woodpecker, the Hairy Woodpecker is noticeably larger with a longer bill. A rough guideline: The downy's bill is about half the length of its head while the hairy's bill

is nearly the length of its head. The Hairy Woodpecker is also not as common around human habitation, especially in urban and suburban areas. During spring courtship, listen for the hairy's staccato drumming and *wicky-wicky-wicky* call. The hairy is found over most of the state, except for treeless areas of eastern Colorado.

*Female*

family: WOODPECKER

*Colaptes auratus*

**Field ID:** Gray back speckled with black; black crescent on the chest; white rump; rusty-red wing linings. The male has a bright red cheek stripe, or "mustache." **Size:** 12½ inches.

**Habitat:** Lowland riparian woodlands; mountain aspen and coniferous forests; piñon-juniper woodlands; urban and suburban landscaping.

**Field Notes:** Flickers are the most familiar and ubiquitous of woodpeckers, as common in cities, suburbs, parks, and yards as they are in the woods. Their loud *yuk yuk yuk* call boldly announces that a flicker is in residence. Watch for the white flash of the flicker's rump and its reddish wings when it flies, its flight pattern characteristically dipping and undulating. The red-shafted form is most common in Colorado, with occasional sightings of **Yellow-shafted Flickers** on the eastern plains, most of which are probably hybrids of the two forms. The flicker is found throughout the state.

family: WOODPECKER

Mary Taylor Gray's Colorado Birding Tip
**Eastern Plains: A Place of Meeting**

Colorado's eastern plains are a melting pot of sorts, where species and races of birds found mainly in the eastern United States are sometimes seen alongside their western cousins. Wooded stream and river corridors, ponds, and reservoirs are good places to check for the yellow-shafted race of Northern Flicker, Red-headed and Red-bellied Woodpeckers, Baltimore Orioles, Eastern Towhees, Rose-breasted Grosbeaks, American Redstarts, Gray Catbirds, Northern Cardinals, a variety of warblers, and other species. Watch in open country for Dickcissels, Eastern Meadowlarks, Eastern Bluebirds, and Bobolinks.

# WESTERN WOOD-PEWEE

*Contopus sordidulus*

**Field ID:** Olive-gray with paler undersides; peaked head; two narrow, white wing bars. **Size:** 6¼ inches.

**Habitat:** Mountain coniferous forests, particularly ponderosa pine; aspen and piñon-juniper woodlands; riparian areas; urban and suburban areas.

**Field Notes:** Like most of the small flycatchers, the Western Wood-Pewee is rather unremarkable in appearance, but its loud call—a nasal *peer*, descending slightly in pitch—is distinctive if not pretty. Wood-pewees are common and not shy, allowing you to walk right beneath the tree where they perch to get a good look and listen. In summer they range from the eastern foothills west throughout the state and along major river drainages of the eastern plains. A close cousin, the **Olive-sided Flycatcher**, is darker and larger and an uncommon summer breeder in our state.

*Olive-sided Flycatcher*

*Sayornis saya*

**Field ID:** Brownish-gray with paler undersides; black tail; cinnamon belly. **Size:** 7½ inches.

**Habitat:** Grasslands; shrublands; open country.

**Field Notes:** This familiar flycatcher is a common summer visitor to lower elevations across Colorado, easily identified by its size and cinnamon belly. Tolerant of human observers, phoebes perch in full view on fence wires as they pump their tails up and down. This phoebe is named for Thomas Say, a naturalist who explored Colorado in 1820 with the Long Expedition and recorded first sightings of many species.

family: TYRANT FLYCATCHER

Mary Taylor Gray's Colorado Birding Tip
**Canyons of the Eastern Plains**

Many people are surprised to learn that Colorado's eastern plains are cut by deep canyons, especially in the southeastern corner of the state. These sheltered corridors, with their trees and shaded pools, host a wonderful variety of migrating birds each spring. Vogel, Picketwire, and Piñon Canyons on and around the northern parcel of the Comanche National Grasslands, and Carrizo, Cottonwood, and Picture Canyons in the far southeast corner of the state are accessible to the public. Contact the U.S. Forest Service, Comanche National Grasslands, for more information—719-384-2181 for the northern parcel, 719-523-6591 for the southern parcel.

Jan Feb Mar **Apr May June July Aug Sept** Oct Nov Dec     *147*

# WESTERN KINGBIRD

*Tyrannus verticalis*

family: TYRANT FLYCATCHER

**Field ID:** Soft-gray back, wings, and head; dark tail; sulphur-yellow belly. The outer edges of the tail are white. **Size:** 8¾ inches.

**Habitat:** Grasslands; shrublands; riparian areas; farm and ranch lands; piñon-juniper woodlands; urban and suburban areas.

**Field Notes:** The kingbird belongs to a group known as tyrant flycatchers, an appropriate term for its sometimes aggressive behavior. Kingbirds will dive-bomb hawks and sometimes

drive them from their turf. The kingbird's voice is in keeping with its harridan behavior—a shrill, metallic twitter that sounds like a tape on fast-forward. Kingbirds show up from mid-March through mid-September over much of the state, in grasslands, shrublands, and open country with scattered trees and woodlands. In summer, the similar **Cassin's Kingbird** shows up in foothills and valleys of southeastern Colorado. Its brown tail, which lacks white edges, distinguishes it from the Western Kingbird.

*Cassin's Kingbird*

Jan Feb Mar Apr **May June July Aug Sept** Oct Nov Dec

*Tyrannus tyrannus*

family: TYRANT FLYCATCHER

**Field ID:** Black upperparts; white underparts; distinguishing white edge to the tip of the black tail. **Size:** 8½ inches.

**Habitat:** Riparian areas; farm and ranch land near water; piñon-juniper woodlands; shrublands; urban and suburban areas.

**Field Notes:** The handsome Eastern Kingbird isn't easily confused with any of the other flycatchers. It looks as if it were laid on its back in ink, leaving a white underside and conspicuous white edge to the tip of the black tail. Its head is often "bumped-up" in a cone shape. True to their name, these birds are the "king birds" in their territory and will aggressively drive away intruders. Summer visitors, Eastern Kingbirds are mainly found in eastern Colorado, though they also inhabit western lowlands.

# FLYCATCHERS

The small empidonax flycatchers, known to birders as "empids," are notoriously difficult to identify, presenting the greatest challenge of almost any group of birds seen in Colorado. Classic "LGBs," or little gray birds, they fascinate hard-core birders but may not hold the interest of less involved watchers. Empids are all small, drab, gray-green birds lacking distinctive field marks other than faint eye rings and wing bars. Some similar species may be distinguished only by their calls.

family: TYRANT FLYCATCHER

## WILLOW FLYCATCHER

*Empidonax traillii*
5¾ inches. In summer this flycatcher nests in willow thickets of foothills, valleys, and mountain parks. The dark back is olive-brown with paler breast; white throat; pale yellow belly; and fairly heavy bill. The eye ring is faint or lacking.

## HAMMOND'S FLYCATCHER

*Empidonax hammondii*
5½ inches. This flycatcher is difficult to distinguish from the dusky. It has an olive-gray back; pale gray throat; dark, tiny bill; white eye ring; brownish breast; darker sides; and pale yellow belly. It nests in mature spruce-fir forests of higher mountains where it forages high in the trees, flicking its tail and wings repeatedly. It is often the only empid found in these high forests.

## DUSKY FLYCATCHER

*Empidonax oberholseri*
5¾ inches. This long-tailed flycatcher has an olive-gray back,
pale gray throat, brownish breast,
darker sides, and pale yellow
belly. The eye ring is fairly
prominent. It nests in lower elevation shrublands and woodlands of western valleys, mesas,
and foothills, and eastern plains
near the foothills. Considered
the most common empidonax
flycatcher in the state.

## CORDILLERAN FLYCATCHER

*Empidonax occidentalis*
5½ inches. This empid has an
olive back, yellow throat, olive-
washed breast, yellow belly, and
prominent eye ring that is pointed at the back. It nests in shrublands and woodlands of foothills
and lower mountains.

## GRAY FLYCATCHER

*Empidonax wrightii*
6 inches. This well-named flycatcher is gray with a pale yellow
belly, pale eye ring and wing
bars, and long tail that it pumps
and flicks repeatedly. It inhabits
piñon-juniper habitats mainly in
western foothills and mesas.

family: TYRANT FLYCATCHER

*151*

# ASH-THROATED FLYCATCHER

*Myiarchus cinerascens*

**Field ID:** Gray-brown with pale breast; yellow belly; long tail; pointed head. **Size:** 8½ inches.

**Habitat:** Piñon-juniper and riparian woodlands.

**Field Notes:** With its crest-shaped head, large size, and yellow-washed belly, the ash-throated is a fairly easy flycatcher to identify. It often sits in trees or other exposed perches, sallying forth to catch flying insects and returning to the same perch. This flycatcher is found in summer mainly in piñon-juniper woodlands of southern and western Colorado.

*Perisoreus canadensis*

family: CROW, JAY, and MAGPIE

**Field ID:** Fluffy gray with white throat, forehead, and undersides; dark nape. Young are charcoal-gray all over.
**Size:** 11½ inches.

**Habitat:** High mountain forests, particularly spruce-fir habitat.

**Field Notes:** Often called camp robbers for their larcenous habits, Gray Jays are familiar denizens of picnic areas, camp-grounds, and cabins in mountain coniferous forests throughout the state. These bold opportunists are quite curious and will approach closely, steal tidbits from the picnic table, then slip away to secrecy. Because the Gray Jay does not migrate, it is thickly insulated with feathers, hence its fluffy appearance. Gray Jays move to lower elevations in winter and sometimes visit foothills bird feeders.

*Cyanocitta stelleri*

**Field ID:** Iridescent blue with a black head; striking black crest; white streaking on the forehead. **Size:** 11½ inches.

**Habitat:** Mountain coniferous forests; foothills shrublands; suburban areas.

**Field Notes:** This bold and handsome mountain jay, with its perky pointed crest, is practically the Welcome Wagon bird of the Colorado Rockies. Anyone who visits a high country forest, particularly with picnic basket in hand, soon makes the acquaintance of the Steller's Jay. Though often announcing themselves with loud *shak shak shak* calls, Steller's Jays are quite secretive near their nests. Over much of the state, Steller's Jays favor ponderosa pine and Douglas-fir forests, also inhabiting piñon-juniper and lodgepole pine. In winter they show up at lower elevation foothills feeders.foothills feeders.

Mary Taylor Gray's Colorado Birding Tip
**Camp Robbers**

"Camp robber" is a common nickname used for several crow-family birds renowned for their picnic-mooching skills. Gray Jays, Steller's Jays, Clark's Nutcrackers, and Black-billed Magpies have all been given this apt name. All these assertive birds show up when the picnic basket opens, readily gobble up handouts, steal unattended treats from the picnic table, and have even been known to enter tents seeking food. Though it's tempting, avoid feeding human food to these birds, both for their health and to discourage "tame" behavior among wild birds.

family: CROW, JAY, and MAGPIE

*Cyanocitta cristata*

**Field ID:** Gray-blue back; striking, iridescent-blue wings and tail with white spotting; head crest; black collar. **Size:** 11 inches.

**Habitat:** Urban and suburban areas; and riparian woodlands.

**Field Notes:** A relatively new émigré to Colorado, the eastern Blue Jay has expanded its range westward with the proliferation of trees across the Great Plains. Blue Jays were first seen in Colorado in 1903. They are now well established in eastern Colorado and along the urban corridor of the Front Range, where they are year-round residents, and they're occasionally sighted on the Western Slope. Some Coloradans welcome this strikingly handsome bird, others decry its aggressive nature, particularly at their bird feeders, but no one can ignore the presence of a Blue Jay.

family: CROW, JAY, and MAGPIE

# WESTERN SCRUB-JAY

*Aphelocoma californica*

family: CROW, JAY, and MAGPIE

**Field ID:** Iridescent, electric-blue back, head, and long tail; pale undersides streaked with gray; long, sturdy bill. **Size:** 11½ inches.

**Habitat:** Shrublands and piñon-juniper woodlands of foothills and mesa country.

**Field Notes:** Subtlety is not in the vocabulary of the scrub-jay. Typical of their family, these jays are raucous and rowdy, sounding off with loud *kay kay kay* calls. They adapt well to life around humans and may become fairly tame at picnic and camp-grounds. Scrub-jays are impossible-to-miss, year-round residents of foothills and mesas, especially in western and southern Colorado. They prefer oakbrush habitat. Scrub-jays will come to feeders for seeds, particularly in winter.

*Gymnorhinus cyanocephalus*

**Field ID:** Electric blue all over with some white streaking on the throat. The tail is noticeably shorter than that of the scrub-jay. **Size:** 10½ inches.

**Habitat:** Piñon-juniper woodlands; shrublands; grasslands; mountain forests; riparian areas.

**Field Notes:** Pinyon Jays are interesting members of the crow family, with distinctive habits and behavior. They are very social, living in large flocks that forage about together. As they travel, Pinyon Jays announce their presence with loud mewing calls. Arriving in a noisy, busy group, Pinyon Jays seem to take over a neighborhood like a biker gang taking over the local bar. There is much loud calling, and the group mills around on the ground or in the trees foraging. Eventually they all depart with much fanfare. Pinyon Jays are year-round, though highly mobile, residents of foothills and mesas of southern and western Colorado.

**Jan Feb Mar Apr May June July Aug Sept Oct Nov Dec** *157*

# CLARK'S NUTCRACKER

*Nucifraga columbiana*

**Field ID:** Gray with black wings and tail; long, sturdy bill. The tail is edged in white and the wings show white patches in flight. **Size:** 12 inches.

**Habitat:** High mountain coniferous forests; lower elevation ponderosa and piñon pine woodlands; aspen forests; shrublands.

**Field Notes:** Like its cousin, the Gray Jay, this high mountain jay is an assertive beggar at campgrounds and picnic sites. Particularly striking in flight, the nutcracker flashes bright white patches on its wings and tail, in bold contrast to its black plumage. The nutcracker's voice is particularly harsh, a grating *kraaa!* Named for William Clark of the Lewis and Clark Expedition, nutcrackers are residents of high mountain coniferous forests, wandering into lower elevation woodlands in winter, particularly when ponderosa and piñon nut crops are abundant.

*Pica pica*

**Field ID:** Black head and tail; black and white wings; white underparts; very long tail. The iridescent-black plumage often shines green, blue, and purple in the sun. **Size:** 19 inches; much of the length is in the long tail.

**Habitat:** Cities, towns, and suburbs; riparian areas; agricultural land; grasslands with scattered trees; shrublands; open mountain forests.

**Field Notes:** The magpie, so striking in appearance, always provokes some kind of comment. Boldly marked in black and white, its plumage glimmers with blue, green, and purple in strong light. In flight, the white wing patches flash like semaphore signals. Magpies are somewhat wary of humans but frequently live close to people in urban and suburban areas, exploiting trash and other available food. Magpies prefer open country with trees for nesting. Their large, domed stick nests are easily seen in trees, especially in winter. Magpies live throughout the state year-round.

family: CROW, JAY, and MAGPIE

**Jan Feb Mar Apr May June July Aug Sept Oct Nov Dec**     *159*

*Corvus brachyrhynchos*

**Field ID:** All black with a heavy, powerful beak; in some light the plumage shines an iridescent purple. **Size:** 17½ inches.

**Habitat:** Towns, cities, and suburbs; agricultural and riparian areas; shrublands; grasslands; pine forests.

**Field Notes:** The large size, glossy black plumage, brassy manner, and familiar *caw!* call make the crow one of the best-known birds in America. The crow has expanded its range in recent years and is now quite common in towns and cities as well as in foothills and lower mountains throughout the state. Crows are smaller and more gregarious than ravens. To distinguish a crow from a raven in flight, look for the squared-off tail; the raven's tail ends in a wedge shape.

*Corvus corax*

**Field ID:** Glossy all-black plumage; long, heavy, arched bill; shaggy throat feathers. **Size:** 24 inches.

**Habitat:** Mountain habitats, including forests, cliffs, and meadows; lowland shrublands; grasslands; riparian, agricultural, and suburban areas.

**Field Notes:** This large, black bird offers a dramatic presence in the Colorado high country, silently skimming cliffs, mountains, and high valleys like a black shadow. The raven's hollow *kraw!* often punctuates the air as it soars overhead. A raven is much larger than a crow and its tail ends in a wedge rather than straight across like a crow's. In general, ravens prefer higher elevation habitats while crows are lowland birds, though both species often cross over this generalization—ravens wandering into lower elevations after the nesting season. Crows tend to live closer to human habitation.

*Poecile atricapillus*

CATHY AND GORDON ILLG

**Field ID:** Gray with buffy sides; whitish face and underparts; black throat and cap. **Size:** 5¼ inches.

**Habitat:** Urban and suburban landscaping; riparian areas; aspen forests; oakbrush; piñon-juniper woodlands.

**Field Notes:** This friendly and energetic bird adapts well to life around humans and is among the most familiar and endearing of songbirds. Like a little wood sprite, the chickadee moves busily about, sounding its buzzing *chick-a-dee-dee* call and two-toned *fee-bee* song. Chickadees can be found throughout the state, from high mountains to riparian areas of the eastern plains to city parks and yards. In fall the mountain-nesting birds move to lower elevations, inhabiting riparian areas and residential landscaping, where they come readily to feeders.

family: TITMOUSE

**Jan Feb Mar Apr May June July Aug Sept Oct Nov Dec**

*Poecile gambeli*

**Field ID:** Gray with white underparts; black cap and throat; white stripe above the eye. **Size:** 5¼ inches.

**Habitat:** Foothills and mountain coniferous and aspen forests; shrublands; riparian areas; urban and suburban landscaping in winter.

**Field Notes:** The white stripe above the eye distinguishes the Mountain Chickadee from its very similar cousin, the Black-capped Chickadee. The Mountain Chickadee echoes the characteristic *chick-a-dee-dee-dee* call, but in a more raspy voice. It whistles a high, clear song easily heard in the mountain forest—*fee-bee-bee*—descending on each note. In winter chickadees move to lower elevations, showing up at feeders in foothills and low-lands near the mountains.

family: TITMOUSE

Mary Taylor Gray's Colorado Birding Tip
### Which Chickadee?

The call of a Black-capped Chickadee is easy to remember—*chick-a-dee-dee*—as is its two-note song, *fee-bee*, which goes down on the second note. In Colorado we have two common chickadees, the black-capped and the mountain, which often share habitats, particularly in the foothills and mountains. Their calls and songs are just different enough to distinguish between the two species by ear. The Black-capped Chickadee sounds the familiar, somewhat buzzy chickadee call, while the voice of the Mountain Chickadee is more hoarse and raspy—*tsik-a-zee-zee*—and its song is a three-beat *fee-bee-bee*, descending on each note.

**Jan Feb Mar Apr May June July Aug Sept Oct Nov Dec**     *163*

# JUNIPER TITMOUSE

*Baeolophus ridgwayi*

**Field ID:** Pale gray with an upright head crest.
**Size:** 5¾ inches.

**Habitat:** Piñon-juniper woodlands; ponderosa pine forests; shrublands; riparian areas.

**Field Notes:** This energetic but nondescript little bird was formerly known as the Plain Titmouse, but it might just as well have been called the "plain-Jane" titmouse, so unremarkable is it save for its perky head crest, which gives the little bird an inquisitive expression. Plain or not, the titmouse is an endearing bird to watch, endowed with such energy and industry it puts a honeybee to shame. The Juniper Titmouse is most often found year-round in mature piñon-juniper woodlands of western and southern Colorado.

*Psaltriparus minimus*

**Field ID:** Gray with paler undersides; short bill; long tail. The male has dark eyes and the female cream-colored eyes. Some males have a black mask around the eyes and are known as "Black-eared" Bushtits. **Size:** 4½ inches.

**Habitat:** Piñon-juniper woodlands; shrublands.

**Field Notes:** A Bushtit is not a flashy bird. Dressed in dove-gray plumage with no defining field marks or colors, it is still a charmer by virtue of its tiny size and its industry. One of the smallest songbirds in North America, the bushtit is also among the busiest. Sociable and friendly, Bushtits flock with other Bushtits, chickadees, titmice, and wrens. After the nesting season, groups of as many as 50 birds may drift through a piñon wood-land, twittering in high-pitched voices. Bushtits live year-round in piñon-juniper forests of southern and western Colorado, wan-dering also through other areas of the state.

**Jan Feb Mar Apr May June July Aug Sept Oct Nov Dec**  *165*

# RED-BREASTED NUTHATCH

*Sitta canadensis*

**Field ID:** Steel-gray back and wings; rusty-red underparts; white head with black cap; black eye stripes. **Size:** 4¼ inches.

**Habitat:** Mountain coniferous forests; oakbrush shrublands; riparian woodlands; urban and suburban landscaping.

**Field Notes:** Nuthatches never fail to delight observers as they travel headfirst down the trunks of trees, poking into cracks and crevices in the bark seeking insects. This unique and comical habit is celebrated in their many whimsical nicknames—"topsy-turvy bird," "devil-down-head." The Red-breasted Nuthatch inhabits Colorado's foothills and mountains year-round, its numbers swelling in some areas when the cyclic pine nut crop is good. In winter many show up at low-elevation feeders.

# WHITE-BREASTED NUTHATCH

*Sitta carolinensis*

**Field ID:** Bluish-gray with white undersides and head; very black cap spreading down the back of the neck. The head flows into the body with little definable neck; the slender bill is often pointed in line with the body. **Size:** 5¾ inches.

**Habitat:** Ponderosa pine and piñon-juniper forests; aspen forests; lowland riparian areas; urban and suburban landscaping.

**Field Notes:** Of Colorado's three nuthatches, the white-breasted is perhaps the easiest to identify thanks to its bright white cheeks contrasting with the narrow black panel across the top of its head. The nuthatch pair raises its family, then stays together on the same small territory through the winter, foraging separately but keeping in touch by calling to each other. Listen for their rapid, high-pitched *yank, yank, yank* call in mountain and lowland forests. White-breasted Nuthatches are found year-round from the foothills of the Eastern Slope west across the state, and sometimes in riparian woodlands along the South Platte and Arkansas Rivers.

Jan Feb Mar Apr May June July Aug Sept Oct Nov Dec

# PYGMY NUTHATCH

*Sitta pygmaea*

family: NUTHATCH

**Field ID:** Blue-gray back and wings; whitish underparts; short tail with white edges; small head; long pointed bill; gray-brown cap that covers the head down to the eye line. **Size:** 4¼ inches.

**Habitat:** Ponderosa pine forests and other coniferous forests.

**Field Notes:** The smallest of the nuthatches and truly a bird of the Colorado mountains, the pygmy lives primarily in ponderosa pine forests where it caches pine nuts as winter provender, though it will make use of other habitats. During the cold months Pygmy Nuthatches gang together and forage in large groups, and roost together in crevices. One hollow pine tree was found to shelter some 150 nuthatches, all huddling together like a brownie troop around the campfire. More than the other nuthatches, Pygmy Nuthatches forage among the outer branches of trees.

# BROWN CREEPER

*Certhia americana*

**Field ID:** Brown overall; streaked and speckled with white; lighter undersides; long rufous-red tail; white line over the eye; very long, sharp, down-curving bill. **Size:** 5¼ inches.

**Habitat:** Mountain coniferous forests; lowland riparian areas; urban and suburban landscaping.

**Field Notes:** While creepers aren't particularly remarkable in appearance, their behavior is quite interesting. Supported by their stiff tails, they busily hop their way up the trunks of trees, peering into crevices, poking into notches using their bills like long, curving tweezers, and spiraling ever-upward as if walking up the side of a wall wearing antigravity boots. They live year-round from Eastern Slope foothills west across the state, moving into urban landscaping and lowland riparian habitats in winter.

Jan Feb Mar Apr May June July Aug Sept Oct Nov Dec

# ROCK WREN

*Salpinctes obsoletus*

**Field ID:** Grayish-brown with small white spots; pale whitish undersides; peachy flanks; cinnamon rump; buffy tips on tail.
**Size:** 6 inches.

**Habitat:** Cliffs and rocky hillsides; bare rocky ground; grasslands; shrubby slopes; riparian and urban areas.

**Field Notes:** Well camouflaged, the Rock Wren's plumage allows it to dissolve against the rugged background of the canyons and rocky slopes where it lives. The Rock Wren's voice, a repetitive whirring song among the rocks, will probably announce the bird before it is seen. Sit quietly and watch the rocks, and the wren will soon hop into sight. Rock Wrens are found in summer from eastern foothills west across the state and in canyon areas of southeastern Colorado.

Jan Feb Mar **Apr May June July Aug Sept Oct** Nov Dec

# CANYON WREN

*Catherpes mexicanus*

**Field ID:** Brownish-red with white throat and breast; chestnut belly; speckled plumage; upcocked tail with black rings.
**Size:** 5¾ inches.

**Habitat:** Cliffs, canyons, and rocky slopes.

**Field Notes:** Many people might think of wrens as birds of marshes and moist woodlands, but the Canyon Wren is a bird of Colorado's cliffs and canyons. Most watchers may need to be satisfied with hearing its voice for the Canyon Wren is small and unremarkable and often not easily seen against its rocky habitat. But the clear notes of its song, cascading down the musical scale, are reward enough. Canyon Wrens live year-round in foothills and canyon country of southern and western Colorado.

family: WREN

Mary Taylor Gray's Colorado Birding Tip
**Song of the Canyon Wren**

The song of the Canyon Wren is among the most beautiful sounds of Colorado's outdoors. Cascading melodiously down the scale like water bubbling down a rocky streambed, the Canyon Wren's song is a perfect musical interpretation of its rock-tumbled habitat. Listen for Canyon Wrens when you are hiking in canyon or mesa country, or wherever rocky cliffs offer appropriate habitat.

Jan Feb Mar Apr May June July Aug Sept Oct Nov Dec     *171*

# BEWICK'S WREN

*Thryomanes bewickii*

**Field ID:** Grayish-brown with pale gray underparts; distinctive white eyebrow; long tail showing black and white beneath.
**Size:** 5¼ inches.

**Habitat:** Piñon-juniper woodlands; shrublands; lowland riparian forests.

**Field Notes:** Pronounced "Buick's," like the automobile, the Bewick's Wren is a bird of shrublands and open piñon-juniper forests, foraging busily into cracks and crevices, its tail flicking nervously side to side or cocked upward in classic wren fashion. Populations of this species have declined greatly in the eastern United States due to deforestation, but are still strong in the West. The Bewick's Wren is found spring through fall mainly in southeastern and western Colorado.

*Troglodytes aedon*

**Field ID:** Grayish-brown with paler undersides; faint barring pattern on plumage; faint eyebrow. **Size:** 4¾ inches.

**Habitat:** Various woodlands, particularly riparian, aspen, and ponderosa pine.

**Field Notes:** This wren is dull and nondescript in appearance, with few distinguishing field marks. But its wonderful voice makes it a delight to encounter. The House Wren's song is a cheery, whistley cascade of notes that seem to go on and on, as if the bird insists you join in its good cheer. House Wrens often take up residence near human habitation and will move readily into a well-placed birdhouse with an opening of one and one-eighth inches. They are found spring through fall over much of the state except for the higher mountains and treeless plains.

# MARSH WREN

*Cistothorus palustris*

**Field ID:** Reddish-brown with paler buffy underparts; white throat; distinctive white eye line; dark brown crown; black upper back streaked with white. **Size:** 5 inches.

**Habitat:** Cattail and bulrush marshes.

**Field Notes:** Though the shy Marsh Wren plays a game of hide-and-seek, it announces its presence with a bright song, the notes bubbling up from among the reeds and cattails of the marsh. Its song is a charming succession of trills, rattles, gurgles, and rasps. Marsh Wrens nest in colonies. They are found only very locally around the state, particularly in the San Luis Valley and in northern Colorado. During winter and migration, they are found along the South Platte and Arkansas Rivers.

*Regulus satrapa*

**Field ID:** Olive-gray washed with yellow; paler underparts; two white wing bars; distinctive white eyebrow with black above it. The crown is yellow in the female, and orange bordered by yellow in the male. **Size:** 4 inches.

**Habitat:** Mountain coniferous forests, especially dense spruce-fir, piñon-juniper, or riparian woodlands; residential landscaping in winter.

**Field Notes:** Like its cousin the Ruby-crowned Kinglet, the golden-crowned looks like a plump doughball with an eye and a sharp bill. It is equally energetic, flicking its wings busily as it moves about high mountain forests in perpetual search of insects. The golden-crowned is less common in Colorado than the ruby-crowned, found in high spruce-fir forests in summer, moving into lowland coniferous and riparian woodlands and urban and suburban parks and gardens in winter. Its voice is very high pitched, sounding like a tape on fast-forward.

family: KINGLET

**Jan Feb Mar Apr May June July Aug Sept Oct Nov Dec**

*Regulus calendula*

**Field ID:** Gray-olive on back and wings; paler and yellow below with two white wing bars; white eye ring. The male's red crown patch is seldom visible.
**Size:** 4¼ inches.

**Habitat:** High mountain coniferous forests; lowland forests in winter.

**Field Notes:** The kinglet is a plump, round dab of a bird. Each large eye is surrounded by a white ring that makes the bird seem to be staring. The kinglet's full-throated warble—a fine, loud sound for such a tiny sprite—enlivens a pine tree or thicket, though the

bird itself may be very hard to find. Ruby-crowneds nest in high mountain forests in summer, moving into lower elevation woodlands, riparian areas, and urban and suburban landscaping during migration and winter.

*Female*

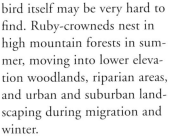

Mary Taylor Gray's Colorado Birding Tip
**A Singing Doughball**

In summer in the moist forests below timberline, a cheery whistling sounds from high among the branches of a subalpine fir. Though his song is distinctive, finding the singer may take some searching, for the Ruby-crowned Kinglet is one of our tiniest songbirds, resembling a gray-green doughball with a beak and big eyes. But his three-phrased song, once heard, is easy to recall using the mnemonic *see, see, see; you, you, you; look at me, look at me, look at me.*

*family:* KINGLET

*Polioptila caerulea*

**Field ID:** *Male:* Blue-gray with pale gray underparts; long tail and bill; white eye ring; black eyebrow in breeding plumage. *Female:* Gray with bluish tones; white eye ring; long tail and bill.
**Size:** 4½ inches.

**Habitat:** Piñon-juniper woodlands; oakbrush, and other shrublands.

**Field Notes:** This tiny bird isn't shy, but its manic behavior—busily flitting back and forth among the branches pursuing flying insects—makes it hard to focus on for long with binoculars. The gnatcatcher makes much use of its tail, flicking it side to side, cocking it up, and fanning it open and closed. The male gnatcatcher sings frequently during breeding season, a high-pitched, buzzy series of notes. The pair's shrill *zeee* calls sound like a conversation among mice. Gnatcatchers are found in summer mainly in southern and western Colorado.

**Female**

family: GNATCATCHER

# AMERICAN DIPPER

*Cinclus mexicanus*

family: DIPPER

**Field ID:** Sooty gray with short tail; long legs; chunky body.
**Size:** 7½ inches.

**Habitat:** Rushing streams and rivers of mountains and foothills.

**Field Notes:** The dipper is without a doubt one of the most unique and curious of Colorado songbirds. Dippers live along mountain streams. They feed on insects, larvae, and other invertebrate prey, jumping in and disappearing underwater in pursuit of their quarry. Dippers, sometimes called water ouzels, have a number of adaptations for underwater hunting. Dippers are found along mountain streams and rivers, moving to lower elevations in foothills and canyons in winter.

Mary Taylor Gray's Colorado Birding Tip
### Underwater Songbird

Ever been hiking along a mountain stream and noticed a little gray bird suddenly jump into the rushing water and disappear beneath the surface? The American Dipper is adapted for a unique underwater hunting technique. It has protective third eyelids that function like dive goggles, dense plumage with water-repellent oil, flaps of skin that close over the nostrils to keep out water, and the ability to "fly" underwater, using its wings to propel itself after insects and other food. Look for dippers along clear, rushing mountain streams statewide.

*Sialia mexicana*

**Field ID:** *Male:* Deep blue with rusty-red breast and back; whitish belly. *Female:* Brownish-gray with a wash of red on her breast and sides.
**Size:** 7 inches.

**Habitat:** Ponderosa pine and piñon-juniper woodlands; oakbrush shrublands; open country adjacent to woodlands.

**Field Notes:** Removal of dead trees, and the proliferation of nonnative cavity-nesters like starlings and house sparrows, have greatly reduced nest habitat for bluebirds. The Bluebird Project, a joint effort between the Colorado Division of Wildlife and the Denver Audubon Society, offers nest boxes for the construction of bluebird "trails," greatly increasing the available nest cavities for all species of bluebirds in Colorado. In summer, Western Bluebirds inhabit foothills and lower mountains across the state, living year-round in southern Colorado. The similar appearing **Eastern Bluebird** can be found regularly in the extreme northeastern corner of the state, with occasional sightings elsewhere.

*Female*

family: THRUSH

*Sialia currucoides*

**Field ID:** *Male:* In the sunlight, the male bluebird is a striking azure blue with a paler breast. *Female:* Gray with a bluish wash. In shadow, bluebirds are a dull gray. **Size:** 7¼ inches.

**Habitat:** Mountain meadows and shrublands adjacent to open woodlands, particularly piñon-juniper and ponderosa pine; aspen forests; shrublands.

**Field Notes:** Bluebirds are one of the delights of the mountain summer, flitting across mountain meadows like scraps of the mountain sky caught in the breeze. The male's amazing blue color is due not to pigment but to special structures on the feathers that reflect and scatter light. Out of the sun, that flashy outfit fades to dull gray. Mountain Bluebirds prefer drier, more open habitat than other bluebirds, usually nesting in trees at the edge of open country. They hover like helicopters in one spot before dropping down on insect prey in the grass. Mountain Bluebirds are found in mountainous habitats statewide in summer and in winter in lower elevations of southern and far western Colorado.

*Female*

family: THRUSH

# TOWNSEND'S SOLITAIRE

*Myadestes townsendi*

**Field ID:** Dark gray with paler underparts; buffy wing patches; white eye ring; long tail. **Size:** 8½ inches.

**Habitat:** Coniferous forests.

**Field Notes:** The Townsend's Solitaire is not a bird to attract a lot of attention, though its single, high-pitched, piping call note is quite distinctive, sounding across its forest habitat. The solitaire's song is typical of the thrush family, a cheery series of fluting whistles. Solitaires usually perch at the tops of trees, though they will flush if approached too boldly. Solitaires live year-round in Colorado's foothills and mountains, moving higher in the summer and down to lower elevations in winter.

family: THRUSH

# SWAINSON'S THRUSH

*Catharus ustulatus*

**Field ID:** Warm olive with streaky spotted breast; buffy eye ring. **Size:** 7 inches.

**Habitat:** Streamside thickets of foothills and lower mountains; watered ravines.

**Field Notes:** With its charming, fluting song, characteristic of the thrush family, this small, spotted-breasted thrush can be difficult to distinguish from other thrushes, such as the Hermit Thrush. Its song is a series of whistles that rise in pitch. The Swainson's Thrush breeds in the mountains and migrates through eastern Colorado foothills and riparian habitats.

Jan Feb Mar Apr **May June July Aug Sept** Oct Nov Dec

*Catharus guttatus*

**Field ID:** Brown with reddish tail; spotted white breast; somewhat resembling an immature robin. **Size:** 6¾ inches.

**Habitat:** High mountain coniferous forests, particularly spruce-fir habitats.

**Field Notes:** Like many adult thrushes, this small cousin of the robin looks somewhat like a juvenile robin due to its spotted breast. Countless Colorado hikers know the song yet have never seen the singer, as the Hermit Thrush is well named—a shy and secretive bird that shuns attention. Hermit Thrushes are found throughout the Colorado high country in summer and statewide during migration.

family: THRUSH

Mary Taylor Gray's Colorado Birding Tip
**Music of the Hermit Thrush**

High in Colorado's subalpine forest in summer, an unseen singer performs a wondrous song. The clear, bell-like tones of the Hermit Thrush carry through the trees, the first melodic phrase repeated at a different pitch. The notes of the Hermit Thrush are especially rich and resonant. But the singer itself is shy, a forest ventriloquist who has led many an entranced listener on a fruitless search for the source of the Hermit Thrush's song.

Jan Feb Mar Apr **May June July Aug Sept Oct** Nov Dec

# AMERICAN ROBIN

*Turdus migratorius*

**Field ID:** Dark gray with bright "robin-red" breast and white eye ring. The female's breast is duller than the male's. The juvenile bird has a paler, spotted breast. **Size:** 10 inches.

**Habitat:** A variety of habitats statewide, including mountain forests; towns, cities, and suburbs; riparian areas; and agricultural areas.

**Field Notes:** This most familiar of songbirds needs little introduction. Robins have been memorialized in folklore and song, revered as a symbol of the return of spring, announced with their *cheer-up, cheer-up* call. Many robins, however, spend winter in Colorado, feeding on juniper berries, Russian olives, and other berries and fruits. They are also abundant summer residents of mountains, valleys, agricultural lands, and urban and suburban areas.

# NORTHERN MOCKINGBIRD

*Mimus polyglottos*

**Field ID:** Gray above; paler gray below; long bill and tail. Prominent white patches on the wings and white tail edges are visible in flight. **Size:** 10 inches.

**Habitat:** Piñon-juniper woodlands; farm and ranch land; riparian areas; shrublands; grasslands.

**Field Notes:** The mockingbird is easily outclassed by other birds in the flashy plumage department, but it wins hands down for versatility in its vocal repertoire. Its Latin name means "many-tongued mimic." Watch for the flash of white wing patches and the white edges of the tail when the mockingbird flies. Mockingbirds are found in summer and during migration mostly in eastern Colorado, concentrated in the southeast. A close cousin, the **Gray Catbird**, shows up along the South Platte and Arkansas Rivers during migration, with some summer visitors along the edge of the Front Range. It is dark gray with a black cap and chestnut patch under the tail.

***Gray Catbird***

**Jan Feb Mar Apr May June July Aug Sept Oct Nov Dec**

# SAGE THRASHER

*Oreoscoptes montanus*

**Field ID:** Brownish-gray with heavily streaked, buffy underparts; straight bill; white corner patches on tail; two white wing bars. **Size:** 8½ inches.

**Habitat:** Sagebrush shrublands; farm and ranch land; grasslands; piñon-juniper woodlands.

**Field Notes:** The thrasher's drab appearance matches its arid habitats, so it's surprising to discover it has the musical voice usually associated with bright songbirds. But thrashers belong to a family of avian vocal stylists, the mockingbirds. The Sage Thrasher's song is a cheery series of rich warbling. The Sage Thrasher, often seen on the ground, disappears quickly beneath a shrub if alarmed. It is common in summer in the sagebrush-covered foothills and mesas of northern Colorado as well as in the San Luis Valley.

# BROWN THRASHER

*Toxostoma rufum*

**Field ID:** Rich reddish-brown with buffy, heavily streaked underparts; yellow eye; curved bill. **Size:** 11½ inches.

**Habitat:** Lowland riparian woodlands; shrublands; suburban areas.

**Field Notes:** The Brown Thrasher transcends its brown appearance with a song that is melodious and a delight for listeners. Usually secretive, in spring the male thrasher adopts a conspicuous song perch atop a shrub and begins his innovative song, mimicking the songs of other birds, changing and adding elements like a composer. He generally repeats song phrases twice. Brown Thrashers are found from spring through fall in riparian areas of the eastern plains, particularly along the South Platte and Arkansas Rivers.

family: MOCKINGBIRD and THRASHER

# HORNED LARK

*Eremophila alpestris*

**Field ID:** Grayish-brown with a pale yellow throat; black chest collar; black stripes on the head; a black "mustache." Its small black "horns" aren't always visible. **Size:** 7¼ inches.

**Habitat:** Alpine tundra; shrublands; stubble fields; pastures, and grasslands.

**Field Notes:** Usually the Horned Lark is not apt to attract a great deal of attention, but the male's spring courtship flight is a marvel to see. Adapted to life in open country where there are few trees, the Horned Lark has evolved a song display, called *larking*, that is performed on the wing. The male carves a series of circles in the sky while filling the air with his bright singing. Finally he folds his wings and plummets earthward, pulling up at the last moment. Horned Larks nest on the alpine tundra and winter in large flocks on the prairie. On one day in 1984, 15,580 were counted at the Pawnee National Grassland in Weld County.

*Anthus rubescens*

**Field ID:** Grayish-brown with buffy underparts; buffy eyebrow; dark brown or black legs. White outer tail feathers are noticeable in flight. **Size:** 6½ inches.

**Habitat:** Tundra; banks of rivers, streams, and canals in winter.

**Field Notes:** Summer hikers on the alpine tundra have likely seen pipits; perhaps without consciously noticing them. Pipits are rather ordinary-looking, slender, brown birds, sparrowlike but with long bills. They walk about on the ground rather than hopping. Pipits flush in small flocks when disturbed. The pipit is one of the few birds that nest on the alpine tundra, particularly in moist areas, migrating to lower elevations in winter and inhabiting the edges of flowing waterways where it can find open water.

Mary Taylor Gray's Colorado Birding Tip
**Birds Above Timberline**

Colorado's alpine tundra is a forbidding place where a snowstorm can blow in unexpectedly even on the hottest August day. Yet several hardy bird species nest on this barren ground. White-tailed Ptarmigan feed on the buds and shoots of alpine willows and nest beneath the sheltering shrubs. Brown-capped Rosy-Finches nest amid the rocks of alpine cliffs. Horned Larks traverse Colorado, spending winter on the prairie and nesting on the tundra. American Pipits favor moist alpine meadows for nesting.

family: WAGTAIL and PIPIT

Jan Feb Mar **Apr** May June July Aug **Sept Oct** Nov Dec

# CEDAR WAXWING

*Bombycilla cedrorum*

**Field ID:** Soft brownish-gray with yellow belly and white under tail; sleek crest; black mask across eyes; yellow tail tip; red wingtips. **Size:** 7¼ inches.

**Habitat:** Riparian areas; urban and suburban landscaping; farm and ranch land; piñon-juniper woodlands.

**Field Notes:** Waxwings are sleek, beautiful birds, and a backyard visit by a group of them is truly a delight. Mainly migration and winter visitors to Colorado, waxwings descend in groups seeking juniper berries and other small fruits, then disappear suddenly. A few waxwings are found here in summer, very locally, mainly in riparian areas of eastern Colorado. The **Bohemian Waxwing** is very similar in appearance, though slightly larger with a gray belly and chestnut undertail area. Its wings have yellow and white spots and a white patch conspicuous in flight.

*Bohemian Waxwing*

Jan Feb Mar Apr May June July Aug Sept Oct Nov Dec

*Lanius ludovicianus*

**Field ID:** Dove-gray with white breast and belly; black tail; white outer feathers. A black mask covers the eyes. The bill is hooked, and in flight the black wings flash a white patch.
**Size:** 9 inches.

**Habitat:** Grasslands; shrublands; farm and ranch land; piñon-juniper woodlands; riparian areas.

**Field Notes:** Shrikes are in a class by themselves, songbirds that are fierce predators and act at times like raptors, hunting mice, small birds, reptiles, and insects. They lack the killing talons of the hawks, but their feet are quite strong with sharp claws. Shrikes use their sharp, hooked bills to bite the necks of their prey. Loggerhead Shrikes are sometimes confused with mockingbirds since they are both gray birds that flash white wing patches in flight. Look for the shrike's black eye mask and hooked bill. Intolerant of human disturbance, shrikes have declined significantly over much of North America. The **Northern Shrike** moves into Colorado in winter, especially onto the northeastern plains. It has a sharply hooked bill, a narrow mask that does not extend above the eye, and its plumage is often barred underneath.

family: SHRIKE

# BELL'S VIREO

*Vireo bellii*

**Field ID:** Grayish-olive back with yellowish underparts; faint white spectacles; two faint, white wingbars. **Size:** 4¾ inches.

**Habitat:** Lowland riparian areas with dense shrubby growth; urban and suburban areas.

**Field Notes:** The Bell's Vireo is a tiny bird whose numbers are declining because of loss of its shrubby, riparian habitat, as well as nest parasitism by a much larger bird, the Brown-headed Cowbird. The cowbird lays its large eggs in the vireo's nest. The cowbird young hatch before the young vireos, and thus receive all the parental care. Bell's Vireos are found in summer along the South Platte River in extreme northeastern Colorado.

*Vireo plumbeus*

**Field ID:** Dark gray back; paler underparts; bold white spectacles; two white wing bars. **Size:** 5½ inches.

**Habitat:** Piñon-juniper, ponderosa pine, and aspen forests; foothills riparian woodlands; oakbrush with scattered tall trees.

**Field Notes:** Tiny and cloaked in gray, the Plumbeous Vireo does not stand out in a crowd, though its white spectacles are quite noticeable. The best way to locate this industrious vireo is by its call. The deliberate *chu-weet, chu-wir, chu-weet* phrases, a bit robinlike, are shorter than the long, melodious song of the Warbling Vireo. The plumbeous was formerly known as the Solitary Vireo. That old species has now been split into three— plumbeous, Cassin's, and blue-headed. The Plumbeous Vireo is fairly common in summer in foothills and lower mountains statewide.

family: VIREO

*Vireo gilvus*

**family: VIREO**

**Field ID:** Olive-gray with whitish underparts washed with yellow; white eyebrow. **Size:** 5½ inches.

**Habitat:** Aspen forests; foothills and lowland riparian woodlands; urban and suburban landscaping.

**Field Notes:** The Warbling Vireo is a common summer inhabitant of woodlands in the foothills and lower mountains across the state. Unremarkable in appearance, it is quite shy and not very cooperative with inquisitive birders. The Warbling Vireo is best recognized by its melodious song, a prolonged series of whistled warbles, that has been described as "a ripple of melody." Male vireos sing from the nest.

# ORANGE-CROWNED WARBLER

*Vermivora celata*

**Field ID:** Yellowish-olive with paler, faintly streaked under-parts. The dark burnt-orange crown is almost impossible to see in the field. **Size:** 5 inches.

**Habitat:** Oakbrush shrublands; foothills riparian areas; aspen and piñon-juniper forests; mountain willow thickets.

**Field Notes:** The Orange-crowned Warbler is another drab, greenish warbler with no distinguishing field marks other than its very active habits. It lives in shrublands and open woodlands of foothills and lower mountains of western Colorado during the summer. It is found statewide during migration. Its song is a high-pitched trill that trails off. The bird's orange crown is often invisible in the field.

family: WOOD-WARBLER

*Vermivora virginiae*

**Field ID:** Gray with yellow breast; white belly; yellow under-tail coverts; prominent white eye ring. **Size:** 4¾ inches.

**Habitat:** Dense, hilly shrublands; riparian thickets; ponderosa pine and piñon-juniper woodlands with shrubby understories; riparian urban and suburban landscaping during migration.

**Field Notes:** The drab appearance and shy habits of the Virginia's Warbler seem in keeping with the dry hillsides of dense oakbrush or other shrubby thickets that it inhabits. One might think the Virginia's Warbler should be an eastern species, but it is a bird of the Southwest, inhabiting Colorado, New Mexico, Arizona, and Utah. It was named for the wife of an army surgeon who first identified it at an Army post in New Mexico in the 1850s. The Virginia's Warbler is fairly common in foothills of the Eastern Slope and in mesa country of western Colorado.

Jan Feb Mar Apr **May June July Aug Sept** Oct Nov Dec

*Dendroica petechia*

**Field ID:** Bright yellow with an olive wash to the back, wings, and tail. The male has reddish streaks on his underside.
**Size:** 5 inches.

**Habitat:** Lowland riparian areas; foothills; urban, suburban, and agricultural landscaping; mountain willow thickets.

**Field Notes:** The Yellow Warbler is a delight both for its bright color and its energy. Flitting about among the outer branches of trees like a scrap of sunshine, the Yellow Warbler works busily through the foliage, picking insects from leaves and twigs. *"Sweet-sweet-sweet, I'm so sweet"* is the classic interpretation of the Yellow Warbler's cheery song. It is found statewide, late spring through early fall.

family: WOOD-WARBLER

Mary Taylor Gray's Colorado Birding Tip
**Mountain Birds**

Summer visitors to Colorado's high country will find that a variety of colorful birds have joined them for the season. Pine Grosbeaks, Red Crossbills, Williamson's and Red-naped Sapsuckers, Pygmy Nuthatches, Lazuli Buntings, and Western Tanagers haunt coniferous forests. Steller's and Gray Jays and Clark's Nutcrackers show up at picnics. Wilson's and Yellow Warblers flit busily about willow thickets; Mountain and Western Bluebirds hunt insects in mountain meadows; while Broad-tailed, Black-chinned, Rufous, and occasional Calliope Hummingbirds sip from wildflowers and visit feeders.

# YELLOW-RUMPED WARBLER

*Dendroica coronata*

**Field ID:** *Male:*
Charcoal-gray with a
bright yellow or white
throat; yellow crown;
yellow rump; yellow
patch on each side. The
male's plumage is duller
and browner in winter.
*Female:* Similar to the
male but duller.
**Size:** 5½ inches.

**Habitat:** Mountain
coniferous and aspen
forests; riparian areas;
other woodlands during
migration.

**Field Notes:** The yellow-rumped is the most abundant
and widespread warbler in North America. Two subspecies are
found in Colorado and they vary mainly by throat color. **The
Audubon's Warbler**, the western subspecies, is the common form
found in our state. It has a yellow throat. The spruce-fir and pine
forests where it breeds sometimes come busily alive with yellow-
rumps. **The Myrtle
Warbler** has a white
throat and is found mainly
in eastern Colorado dur-
ing migration along river
drainages and in urban
and suburban woodlands.
At one time classified as
separate species, the subspecies interbreed freely
where their ranges meet.

*Female*

# BLACK-THROATED GRAY WARBLER

*Dendroica nigrescens*

**Field ID:** Black-and-white-striped head with black mask across the eye; dark gray back; white underparts streaked with black; black throat; yellow dot in front of the eye. Female is similar but duller. **Size:** 5 inches.

**Habitat:** Piñon-juniper woodlands.

**Field Notes:** The Black-throated Gray Warbler inhabits large, mature piñon-juniper woodlands of southern and western Colorado, sometimes nesting in adjacent ponderosa pines and other conifers and using shrublands and riparian areas during migration. Its streaky, contrasting plumage provides good camouflage. The **Townsend's Warbler**, which is black and yellow with a dark cheek patch bordered by yellow, passes through the state from late summer through fall and from eastern foothills west across the state. Its song is a buzzing *weezy, weezy, weezy, weet.*

*Townsend's Warbler*

*Oporornis tolmiei*

family: WOOD-WARBLER

**Field ID:** *Male:* Olive-green with yellowish underparts; blue-gray hood; mottled gray upper breast. *Female:* Paler olive-green with gray hood. Both have white crescents above and below eyes. **Size:** 5¼ inches.

**Habitat:** Riparian shrublands and aspen forests of foothills and montane zones; riparian areas; shrublands; urban and suburban landscaping during migration.

**Field Notes:** The MacGillivray's is a shy and secretive warbler, skulking about in dense vegetation. This warbler is often hard to see amid the willow thickets, log jumbles, and tangles of new growth along the mountain streams it favors. Listen for its sharp *tsik* call note or its song, a buzzy trill that slurs down at the end. In summer the MacGillivray's Warbler breeds across foothills and lower mountains of the state.

# COMMON YELLOWTHROAT

*Geothlypis trichas*

**Field ID:** *Male:* Olive-green with a black bandit's mask across the eyes; whitish brow stripe; bright yellow throat and breast. *Female:* Olive with some yellow on the throat; no mask. **Size:** 5 inches.

**Habitat:** Riparian areas and cattail marshes.

**Field Notes:** A summer visit to any marshy or riparian area, particularly in eastern Colorado, the San Luis Valley, or in lower elevation western valleys, will likely produce an encounter with the Common Yellowthroat, a scrap of yellow darting amongst the greenery. Even if the bird itself is tough to spot, no attentive listener is likely to miss its song. Though usually shy, during spring and summer the male adopts a song perch atop a cattail or in a tree and sings a perky, repetitive *wichity wichity wich.*

*Female*

# WILSON'S WARBLER

*Wilsonia pusilla*

**Field ID:** *Male:* Olive-green on back and wings; yellow underparts; prominent black cap. *Female:* Similar to male but with a cap that is much more drab or even nonexistent.
**Size:** 4¾ inches.

**Habitat:** Mountain willow thickets, from montane zone to above timberline; lower elevation riparian areas; urban and suburban landscaping during migration.

**Field Notes:** The Wilson's Warbler flits among streamside thickets, bringing a bright spot of sunshine to the woodlands. These warblers are generally easily visible because they aren't shy of humans and hunt the outside branches of shrubs and thickets instead of the upper canopy of tall trees. During migration Wilson's Warblers may visit urban parks and foliage and low-elevation riparian areas, but they prefer to nest in the high mountains, even at elevations of 10,000 feet or more.

*Female*

# YELLOW-BREASTED CHAT

*Icteria virens*

**Field ID:** Greenish-gray with white spectacles; white whiskers; bright-yellow throat and breast; white belly. **Size:** 7½ inches.

**Habitat:** Low-elevation and foothills riparian areas; shrublands.

**Field Notes:** The chat is a behemoth amongst the warbler family. While most warblers are bright little birds measuring perhaps 4½ to 5½ inches, this largest of all warblers is a whopping 7½ inches, often leading to confusion in identification. Despite its size and bright yellow breast, the chat is shy and may be hard to see except during spring when the male sings conspicuously. The chat visits Colorado from mid-spring through early fall along riparian areas of the eastern plains and foothills, the San Luis Valley, and western valleys.

Jan Feb Mar Apr **May June July Aug Sept** Oct Nov Dec

# WESTERN TANAGER

*Piranga ludoviciana*

**Field ID:** *Male:* Bright yellow body; bright red head; black wings, back, and tail. *Female:* Dull olive-yellow. **Size:** 7 inches.

**Habitat:** Mountain coniferous forests, especially ponderosa pine and Douglas-fir; oakbrush; piñon-juniper woodlands; aspen forests.

**Field Notes:** Western Tanagers are among the most colorful and welcome birds to spend summer in the Colorado Rockies, the bright yellow, red, and black of their plumage a delight to spot amid the dark green of a pine woodland. Tanagers usually

nest in foothills and lower elevation mountain forests of ponderosa pine, Douglas-fir, scrub oak, or piñon-juniper. The tanager's song sounds like a hoarse robin.

*Female*

Jan Feb Mar Apr **May June July Aug Sept** Oct Nov Dec

*Pheucticus melanocephalus*

**Field ID:** *Male:* Orange with a black head; black and white tail and wings; yellow belly; heavy, whitish bill. *Female:* Buffy with black streaks on the head and back; white stripes around the eyes; heavy bill. **Size:** 8¼ inches.

**Habitat:** Foothills riparian, ponderosa pine, and aspen forests; piñon-juniper woodlands; oakbrush.

**Field Notes:** The heavy, oversized "grosbeak" of this large seed-eating bird is a giveaway, coupled with the striking orange, black, and white plumage of the male. He often sits on the uppermost twig of a tree, his Halloween plumage in bright contrast to the blue sky, singing a clear, whistling song much like a robin's. Black-headed Grosbeaks are found in mountain areas of the state throughout the summer.

*Female*

family: GROSBEAK

*Guiraca caerulea*

**Field ID:** *Male:* Dark blue; chestnut bars on the wings. *Female:* Dull brown with blue highlights; chestnut wing bars. Both have the thick, heavy, grosbeak bill. **Size:** 6¾ inches.

**Habitat:** Lowland riparian areas; weedy edges of ranch land and farmland; shrublands.

**Field Notes:** In the right light, the male Blue Grosbeak is a beautiful sight, gleaming a rich sapphire blue. His heavy grosbeak bill helps distinguish him from other blue birds. The Blue Grosbeak is smaller and less plump than the Black-headed Grosbeak and prefers lower elevation habitats. It is found mainly in eastern Colorado, especially in the southeastern corner of the state.

***Female***

family: GROSBEAK

*Passerina amoena*

**Field ID:** *Male:* Azure-blue head, back, and throat; white belly; cinnamon-red breast; two white wing bars. *Female:* Gray-brown with a bluish wash to her wings, rump, and tail. **Size:** 5½ inches.

**Habitat:** Oakbrush; shrublands; lowland and foothills riparian forests; meadows; piñon-juniper woodlands.

**Field Notes:** The Lazuli Bunting is a fine sight as it flashes red, white, and blue plumage amid the dull vegetation of a brushy hillside. Its colors aren't quite those of the flag, but are striking nonetheless. The bunting's color pattern is similar to a Western Bluebird—blue back, red breast—but the hues differ. The bluebird is a deeper blue and its breast more brick-red. The Lazuli Bunting is a welcome summer visitor to foothills and lowland shrublands and open woodlands over much of the state.

*Female*

family: BUNTING

*Pipilo chlorurus*

**Field ID:** Greenish with grayish underparts; rusty-red cap; white chin; long tail. **Size:** 7¼ inches.

**Habitat:** Hillside and riparian shrublands; piñon-juniper woodlands.

**Field Notes:** The Green-tailed Towhee is quite drab except in the best light, when it acquires a nice greenish sheen. Watch for the distinctive rusty-red cap and long tail that distinguish it from other sparrowlike birds. Rather shy, it may run away into the underbrush, its tail held high like a fleeing chipmunk. This behavior may draw predators away from the nest. It is found in foothills and lower elevation shrublands throughout the state, spring through fall.

*Pipilo maculatus*

**Field ID:** Black head, back, and breast; black wings with white spots; red sides; red eyes; very long tail. Female is similar but duller. **Size:** 8½ inches.

**Habitat:** Oakbrush; piñon-juniper woodlands; riparian areas; urban and suburban landscaping during migration.

**Field Notes:** Towhees are scufflers, noisily and vigorously shuffling their feet in leaf litter and undergrowth, seeking insects and other food. The Spotted Towhee's song is a version of the Eastern Towhee's classic *drink your teeeee* refrain. Towhees are ready singers, sounding their churring calls from shrub-top song perches, making a colorful, musical sight against the sky. In summer they can be found in shrublands across central, southern, and western Colorado, wintering in the southern part of the state.

family: SPARROW

*Pipilo fuscus*

family: SPARROW

**Field ID:** Drab brown with rufous cap; red spot on breast; long tail. **Size:** 8½ inches.

**Habitat:** Piñon-juniper woodlands and shrublands.

**Field Notes:** The drab Canyon Towhee wins no awards for color or beauty, but it might get the ribbon for amiable personality. Compared with the shy Green-tailed Towhee, the Canyon Towhee is quite friendly, haunting picnic grounds and campgrounds seeking dropped tidbits. Canyon Towhees mate for life and the pair remains year-round on their territory, which in our state is found in the canyon and mesa country of southeastern Colorado. Canyon Towhees and their West Coast counterpart, the California Towhee, were once classified as one species, the Brown Towhee.

*Chondestes grammacus*

**Field ID:** Red-brown back streaked with black; plain gray breast with central spot; striking chestnut and black bridle pattern on face and head. White tail corners are very evident in flight. **Size:** 6½ inches.

**Habitat:** Grasslands; shrublands; riparian areas; farm and ranch land.

**Field Notes:** The Lark Sparrow seems like just another drab sparrow until focused within the binoculars. Then the handsome pattern of black and chestnut on its head and face is easily seen. Lark Sparrows feed on the ground among the grass and weeds of open country, often in large flocks. When they flush, the white corners of their tails flash. Lark Sparrows are mainly found on the eastern plains and in the open country of far western Colorado from spring through fall.

family: SPARROW

The sameness of size and color among species makes many sparrows difficult and challenging to identify. Some general characteristics that will help narrow the field are whether a bird has a streaked or plain breast, a spot on the breast, eye rings, or white on the outer tail feathers. Habitat is also useful in identification.

### CASSIN'S SPARROW
*Aimophila cassinii*
6 inches. The Cassin's Sparrow has a brown-streaked gray back and a plain gray breast. It is found in summer in sand sage and rabbitbrush shrublands of eastern Colorado—especially in the southeast corner of the state. White tail corners are visible in flight.

### AMERICAN TREE
### SPARROW  *Spizella arborea*
6¼ inches. The single spot on a clear gray breast, as well as the rufous crown and red-streaked back, helps identify the tree sparrow—an abundant winter visitor. The two-toned bill is yellow below, and dark above. It inhabits old fields, shrublands, farm and ranch land, and riparian areas statewide—particularly in eastern Colorado.

### BREWER'S SPARROW
*Spizella breweri*
5½ inches. This gray-brown sparrow has a plain breast, bold white eye ring, and faint cheek patch. Its trilling, bubbly song is canarylike. It is a common summer inhabitant of the foothills and mesas of western Colorado, particularly in sage-brush shrublands, as well as in the San Luis Valley, and North and Middle Parks.

### VESPER SPARROW
*Pooecetes gramineus*
6¼ inches. The Vesper Sparrow is a common summer inhabitant of grasslands, shrublands, and piñon-juniper woodlands of foothills and mountain parks. It is found statewide, particularly in eastern Colorado, during migration. It is heavily streaked, with white tail edges visible in flight.

## SAGE SPARROW
*Amphispiza belli*

6¼ inches. The Sage Sparrow nests in sagebrush shrublands of the San Luis Valley and in the mesa country of western Colorado. Despite its name, it is found only very locally in sagebrush habitat rather than being broadly distributed. This sparrow is streaky brown with a pale gray head, white eyebrow, white mustache, and dark breast spot.

## SAVANNAH SPARROW
*Passerculus sandwichensis*

5½ inches. A heavily streaked sparrow with a yellow eyebrow and streaking on the breast that sometimes merges into a spot. This sparrow is common in summer in mountain parks and valleys, in the San Luis Valley, and along the South Platte River drainage.

## GRASSHOPPER SPARROW
*Ammodramus savannarum*

5 inches. Another streaky brown sparrow with a plain breast, the Grasshopper Sparrow nests in the grasslands of eastern Colorado, where it may be abundant in specific locales.

## LINCOLN'S SPARROW
*Melospiza lincolnii*

5¾ inches. This high-meadow nesting sparrow is found in willow thickets, meadows, and timberline krummholz forests with adjacent willows throughout western Colorado from late spring through early fall. Its streaked brown back contrasts with a buffy, finely streaked breast and plain, pale belly. The rufous crown has a gray central stripe.

## HARRIS'S SPARROW
*Zonotrichia querula*

7½ inches. This large sparrow can be fairly common during migration and in winter in extreme eastern Colorado—particularly in brushy habitat along the South Platte and Arkansas Rivers. Its black crown, face, and bib are distinctive. The back is a streaked brown.

family: SPARROW

*Calamospiza melanocorys*

**Field ID:** *Male:* All black with white wing patches. *Female:* Streaky gray-brown with white patches on brown wings.
**Size:** 7 inches.

**Habitat:** Shortgrass prairie; farm and ranch land; sagebrush shrublands.

**Field Notes:** The Lark Bunting is Colorado's state bird, an honor many birders question, citing the many more colorful and exciting birds that inhabit our state. The male is quite striking when he flashes white wing patches in contrast to his coal-black plumage. Particularly impressive during his spring courtship flight, he wings up into the sky and gently floats down in a spiral

like a butterfly, singing for all he's worth. Lark Bunting numbers declined severely with loss of shortgrass prairie habitat. They are mainly found in eastern Colorado spring through fall.

*Female*

Jan Feb Mar Apr **May June July Aug Sept** Oct Nov Dec

family: SPARROW

*Spizella passerina*

**Field ID:** Streaky brown with plain gray breast; rufous crown; white eyebrow; black eye line. In winter the plumage fades and the crown becomes brown, streaked with black. **Size:** 5½ inches.

**Habitat:** Ponderosa pine, piñon-juniper, riparian woodlands, and other mountain forests; shrublands; weedy fields; grasslands; urban areas during migration.

**Field Notes:** The rufous-red crown and black eye line identify the very common Chipping Sparrow. Chipping Sparrows are found throughout the state during migration and in the western half of Colorado during summer. The nondescript **Clay-colored Sparrow** is an abundant migrant on the eastern plains—750 were counted one May day at Bonny Reservoir. It is gray with faint streaking, plain breast, and whitish eyebrows.

*Clay-colored Sparrow*

family: SPARROW

*Melospiza melodia*

**Field ID:** Streaked brown back and wings; streaked pale breast with a dark central spot; gray eyebrows; stripes from the corner of the mouth down the neck. **Size:** 6¼ inches.

**Habitat:** Riparian willow thickets; cattail marshes; streamside vegetation.

**Field Notes:** Though it seems like just another streaky brown sparrow, the Song Sparrow endears itself to birders with its cheery song and its hardiness. Song Sparrows live year-round in our state, inhabiting riparian thickets and streamside vegetation, where their rich song—beginning with a few notes, then spilling into a bright warble—can be heard throughout the year. The rufous head-stripes and spot on the breast also help identify the Song Sparrow.

family: SPARROW

*Zonotrichia leucophrys*

**Field ID:** Gray-brown with a pinkish bill; black head, boldly striped in white. **Size:** 7 inches.

**Habitat:** Lowland and mountain willow thickets; streamside vegetation; timberline krummholz woodlands.

**Field Notes:** This large sparrow is one of the most familiar and identifiable of this family of "little gray birds," with its bold black and white striped head. Whether along a prairie stream in winter or in a subalpine meadow in summer, the white-crown is a familiar and companionable Coloradan. Listen for its *jip, jip* call note and its song, a whistling trill.

family: SPARROW

**Jan Feb Mar Apr May June July Aug Sept Oct Nov Dec**   *217*

*Junco hyemalis*

*Oregon form*

*Gray-headed form*

*Slate-colored form*

*Pink-sided form*

**family: SPARROW**

**Field ID:** Five different forms of junco are found in Colorado, all different in appearance. The Oregon form has a dark blue-black cowl covering head and neck; rusty back; rosy sides; and gray wings and tail. The gray-headed comes with light gray head and sides and rusty-red back. The slate-colored is slate gray with a pale belly, and the white-winged is slate gray with white wing bars and white on the tail. The pink-sided, a phase of the Oregon form, has a paler cowl and pink sides. All juncos have white tail edges visible in flight and dark smudges around the eyes. **Size:** 6¼ inches.

**Habitat:** Mountain forests; riparian areas; shrublands; urban and suburban landscaping.

**Field Notes:** The Dark-eyed Junco proves the difficulty of neatly categorizing and labeling birds. Presently, the five different forms of junco, which are quite different from one another in appearance, are classified as one species. The gray-headed, Oregon, and pink-sided are the most common in Colorado, though only the gray-headed nests here during summer in mountain coniferous and aspen forests. The others arrive in fall from more northern areas to spend the winter with us, showing up at lowland feeders.

Mary Taylor Gray's Colorado Birding Tip
**The Many Flavors of Junco**

The Dark-eyed Junco is a handsome little bird that reminds us of the difficulty of imposing human rules of order onto the natural world. The uninitiated would never think the five different forms of junco—Oregon, gray-headed, slate-colored, white-winged, and pink-sided—were all one species. In the past, biologists have classified them separately. But they interbreed, so for now all five of these different-looking birds are lumped together as the Dark-eyed Junco.

**Jan Feb Mar Apr May June July Aug Sept Oct Nov Dec**

*Calcarius mccownii*

**Field ID:** *Breeding plumage—Male:* Gray-brown back flecked with black; pale head with black crown and whiskers; black crescent on breast; chestnut wing patch. *Female:* Buffy-gray streaked with black; streaked crown; faint wing patch. In both sexes, the white tail is marked by an inverted black T. **Size:** 6 inches.

**Habitat:** Shortgrass prairie and rangeland.

**Field Notes:** The pasture land and remnant shortgrass prairie of Weld and Yuma Counties in northeastern Colorado comprise the southernmost breeding range of the McCown's Longspur. The McCown's prefers shorter vegetation than other longspurs and can be found in heavily grazed pastures. It can be abundant in summer at the Pawnee National Grassland and during migration on the extreme eastern plains.

family: SPARROW

Mary Taylor Gray's Colorado Birding Tip
### Sky Dancers of the Prairie

With few trees to provide song perches, songbirds that nest in the prairies, grasslands, and agricultural lands of eastern Colorado have evolved song flights as a means of strutting their stuff during spring courtship. Lark Buntings, Horned Larks, Cassin's Sparrows, Western Meadowlarks, and McCown's and Chestnut-collared Longspurs all perform a delightful song and dance act, called larking, in which they wing high in the sky, singing melodiously, then float or dive back to earth. Each species' flight is unique and the Pawnee National Grassland is a good place to watch for these displays in spring and early summer.

*Calcarius lapponicus*

**Field ID:** *Winter plumage:* Streaked brown, black, and chestnut plumage; white belly and undertail coverts; buffy cheeks and eyebrow; streaked crown. **Size:** 6¼ inches.

**Habitat:** Shortgrass prairie, stubble fields, and farmland.

**Field Notes:** These longspurs breed on the arctic tundra of the far north, moving south into the continental United States in winter. Unfortunately, the winter plumage they wear during their Colorado visit is a good deal less dramatic than the black head and chestnut collar of the summer breeding season. Lapland Longspurs can be abundant in stubble fields and grasslands of eastern Colorado, and they occasionally show up in mountain parks. Watch flocks of Horned Larks closely, since Lapland Longspurs often flock with them in winter.

**family: SPARROW**

*Calcaruis ornatus*

### Field ID:

*Breeding plumage:* Streaky brown and black back; chestnut collar; white tail marked by triangle at tip; buffy-yellow face; black cap; black and white bars on face.

**Size:** 6 inches.

### Habitat:

Shortgrass prairie and rangeland.

**Field Notes:** Like the McCown's Longspur, the chestnut-collared nests on remnant shortgrass prairie in northeastern Colorado. It can be seen at the Pawnee National Grassland and during migration on the extreme eastern plains. It prefers denser and taller vegetation than the McCown's. In spring the courting male Chestnut-collared Longspur performs a delightful song flight in which he rises up on fluttering wings, circles, and glides down while singing a musical warble. The two-syllable *kittle* call is distinctive.

family: SPARROW

Mary Taylor Gray's Colorado Birding Tip
### Longspurs in Colorado

Remnant patches of shortgrass prairie in Colorado comprise the southernmost breeding range of McCown's and Chestnut-collared Longspurs. The arctic-nesting Lapland Longspur also finds winter habitat here. The Pawnee National Grassland in Weld County is a good place to see these grassland sparrows, named for the long claw or spur on their hind toe. Longspurs have a limited range in the United States, and birders come from all over to see them in Colorado.

*Passer domesticus*

**Field ID:** *Male:* Streaky reddish-brown back; paler underparts; gray cap; black throat; red nape. *Female:* Streaky reddish-brown back; plain pale breast; buffy eye stripe. **Size:** 6¼ inches.

**Habitat:** Cities, towns, and suburbs; agricultural areas.

**Field Notes:** Introduced to the United States in 1850, this European species, often called the English sparrow, has spread across the continent and made itself very much at home in North America. First recorded in Colorado in 1895, it is a well-established, year-round resident throughout the state, and one of the

most common feeder birds in urban and suburban areas. These aggressive sparrows are pests that compete with native species for nest cavities and other resources. They may destroy eggs, or kill nestlings and adult native songbirds.

*Female*

**Jan Feb Mar Apr May June July Aug Sept Oct Nov Dec**

*Dolichonyx oryzivorus*

**Field ID:** *Male:* Black with buffy-white nape; white rump and shoulders. *Female:* Buff with brown streaks on back, sides, and head; dark eye line. **Size:** 7 inches.

**Habitat:** Meadows; hayfields; grasslands and farmland.

**Field Notes:** This striking prairie bird arrives on the northern Great Plains of North America in small flocks each spring. They are found only locally in Colorado. But the pale-helmeted male in his black and white plumage is a delight to see where he does show up in our state. During migration Bobolinks travel through eastern Colorado. Some nest in the northeast corner of the state along the South Platte River, in areas of tallgrass prairie around Boulder, and in hay meadows of the Yampa River Valley in northwestern Colorado. By late summer they have moulted their showy plumage and look like drab sparrows.

family: BLACKBIRD and ORIOLE

# RED-WINGED BLACKBIRD

*Agelaius phoeniceus*

**Field ID:** *Male:* Jet-black with scarlet wing patches edged in yellow. *Female:* Brown with heavily streaked paler breast; whitish eyebrow. **Size:** 8¾ inches.

**Habitat:** Cattail marshes; riparian areas; wet meadows; farmland.

**Field Notes:** Walk near a cattail marsh or wetland and you'll likely be serenaded by the noisy music of Red-winged Blackbirds,

sounding a bit like a discordant symphony of kazoos and triangles. The highly territorial males adopt a song perch and flash their scarlet wing patches. Red-wings are found throughout the state in marshes, wetlands, and practically any moist spot sprouting a few cattails. Though some migrate, many blackbirds find sufficient habitat to stay year-round.

*Female*

**Jan Feb Mar Apr May June July Aug Sept Oct Nov Dec**

*Sturnella neglecta*

**Field ID:** Streaky gray back with bright yellow breast marked by a black, V-shaped collar. White tail edges are evident in flight. **Size:** 9½ inches.

**Habitat:** Grasslands; weedy fields; shrublands.

**Field Notes:** Across Colorado's grasslands, farmland, and open country in spring and summer, the bright and cheery voice of the meadowlark dances like notes from some happy flute. The meadowlark has a distinctive flight pattern—a short, fluttering burst followed by a glide—with short wings, neck, and tail and distinguishing white edges to the tail. Meadowlarks inhabit lowland areas year-round, moving into mountain parks in summer.

Mary Taylor Gray's Colorado Birding Tip
**Song of the Prairie**

Colorado old-timers describe the Western Meadowlark's song as calling *Gee-whiz-whillikers; Oh, yes, I am a pretty little bird;* or *Methodist Prea-cher!* The fluid, melodic notes that greeted the first settlers still enliven the Colorado prairie in spring and summer, seeming to spill across the open country like sunshine. All winter the male meadowlark keeps quiet, but when spring arrives, he seeks a perch atop a fence post or tall weed, throws back his head to expose the bold black chevron on his yellow breast, opens wide his bill, and begins to sing.

family: BLACKBIRD and ORIOLE

**Jan Feb Mar Apr May June July Aug Sept Oct Nov Dec**

*Xanthocephalus xanthocephalus*

**Field ID:** *Male:*
All black; striking
yellow hood and
wing patches that
flash white in flight.
*Female:* Dark
brown; yellow
throat and breast.
**Size:** 9½ inches.

**Habitat:** Cattail
and bulrush marshes
and adjacent riparian
and agricultural
land.

**Field Notes:**
Where there are cattail marshes, there are likely to be
Yellow-headed Blackbirds. The territorial males sit atop bobbing
cattails like bright yellow ornaments among the green vegetation.
Like Red-winged Blackbirds, they nest in colonies among the
reeds, though yellow-heads prefer emergent vegetation over
deeper water. Yellow-heads are found in summer on the eastern
plains and in west-
ern valleys and
mountain parks.

*Female*

*Euphagus cyanocephalus*

**Field ID:** *Male:* Black body with greenish cast; iridescent purplish head; yellow eyes. *Female:* Grayish-olive with dark eyes.
**Size:** 9 inches.

**Habitat:** Grasslands; marshes; riparian areas; farmland; urban and suburban landscaping.

**Field Notes:** Brewer's Blackbirds benefit from the feast of insects, grain, and seeds left in farmers' fields after plowing or harvest. They often follow cattle, picking up the insects kicked up by cloven hooves, sometimes standing atop the animals' backs. After the breeding season, Brewer's flock together with Red-winged Blackbirds, cowbirds, grackles, and even starlings. They are found throughout the state in summer, with some wintering along the South Platte, Arkansas, and Colorado River drainages, though they have been displaced in some areas by the Common Grackle.

*Female*

family: BLACKBIRD and ORIOLE

# COMMON GRACKLE

*Quiscalus quiscula*

**Field ID:** *Male:* All black with iridescent greenish-purple plumage; yellow eyes; long sturdy bill; long tail. *Female:* Dull black with less iridescence and shorter tail. The female is smaller than the male. **Size:** 12½ inches.

**Habitat:** Lowland riparian areas; urban and suburban landscaping; farmland.

**Field Notes:** The Common Grackle didn't used to be very common in Colorado, but in the 20th century expanded across the eastern half of the state, displacing the Brewer's Blackbird in many urban and agricultural areas. Now this big, showy, black bird with the gleaming, iridescent plumage and bold yellow eyes struts around yards and fields in summer. Its discordant voice sounds an amazing variety of harsh squawks and squeaks. The **Great-tailed Grackle**, with a much longer, larger tail, first appeared in the state in 1970 and now shows up in western valleys, mountain parks, and on the eastern plains.

*Great-tailed Grackle*

Jan Feb Mar Apr May June July Aug Sept Oct Nov Dec

*Molothrus ater*

**Field ID:** *Male:* Black body with dark brown head. *Female:* Grayish-brown with faint streaking on breast. **Size:** 7½ inches.

**Habitat:** Grasslands; shrublands; farm and ranch land; meadows; woodlands adjacent to these areas.

**Field Notes:** The unremarkable appearance of the Brown-headed Cowbird offers no clue to the huge impact of this species on other birds. Cowbirds are nest parasites—they lay their eggs in the nests of other birds. The host birds then invest their parenting energy in the early hatching cowbird young while their own brood usually dies. Cowbird parasitism is a big factor in the decline of some populations of songbirds. Its effect is greatly magnified with human-caused change, loss, and fragmentation of native habitats. Cowbird eggs have been found in the nests of 38 different songbird species in Colorado. Cowbirds are found statewide from spring through fall.

family: BLACKBIRD and ORIOLE

# ORCHARD ORIOLE

*Icterus spurius*

**Field ID:** *Male:* Black wings and tail marked with white; black hood; dark burnt-orange underparts and rump. *Female:* Olive-green with yellow underparts and two slender white wing bars. **Size:** 7¼ inches.

**Habitat:** Lowland riparian woodlands.

**Field Notes:** Colorado is at the very far western edge of the range of this handsome black-hooded oriole, which is slowly expanding into Colorado. The first records of its nesting in our state date from the early 1970s. It is mainly found in summer along the South Platte and Arkansas River drainages. Orchard Orioles weave hanging pouch nests, similar to those of the Bullock's Oriole. The Orchard Oriole differs from the Bullock's by its chestnut body and all-black head, back, and chest.

Jan Feb Mar Apr **May June July Aug** Sept Oct Nov Dec

*Icterus bullockii*

**Field ID:** *Male:* Fiery orange with orange face marked by a black eye line; black throat; black crown and nape. Wings have large white patches. *Female:* Olive-yellow with buffy underparts; white wing bars. **Size:** 8¾ inches.

**Habitat:** Lowland riparian areas; urban and suburban landscaping.

**Field Notes:** Bullock's Orioles are delightful additions to riparian woodlands. The flashy males, dressed in Halloween colors of black and bright orange, zip energetically among the branches, pausing in the treetops to break into a volley of whistles and chatters. The hanging, woven-pouch nests are amazing pieces of avian engineering, looking rather like a long sock hanging from the trees. The Bullock's Oriole, western counterpart of the Baltimore Oriole, is found over much of the state from spring through fall.

*Female*

family: BLACKBIRD and ORIOLE

Jan Feb Mar Apr **May June July Aug Sept** Oct Nov Dec

# EUROPEAN STARLING

*Sturnus vulgaris*

**Field ID:** Shiny black plumage that appears greenish and purple in the sun; long, sturdy, yellow bill. In winter the starling's plumage is heavily speckled with gold. **Size:** 8½ inches.

**Habitat:** Cities, towns and suburbs; riparian areas; farm and ranch land.

**Field Notes:** Starlings represent either an incredible success story or a miserable disaster, depending upon your point of view. Introduced in 1890 from Europe, these aggressive, gregarious birds spread across North America and now number in the hundreds of millions. First seen in Colorado in 1937, starlings now out-compete native songbirds for nesting sites and resources and are major nuisances due to the noise and droppings they generate. Their song is a broad repertoire of squawks and squeals and they are accomplished mimics. Starlings gather in large flocks and can be distinguished from blackbirds by their bills and speckled plumage. They are found statewide throughout the year.

*Leucosticte australis*

**Field ID:** *Male:* Brown with dark crown; rosy coloring on wings, sides, belly, and rump. *Female:* Dull grayish-brown overall.
**Size:** 6¼ inches.

**Habitat:** Cliffs above timberline; alpine tundra; mountain meadows; shrublands.

**Field Notes:** This unremarkable little gray-brown bird nests on cliff edges above timberline, foraging across the alpine tundra. High-altitude hikers are familiar with rosy-finches mainly as fluttering flocks of drab birds that flush as they approach, skittering off to land again nearby. Rosy-finches winter in mountain parks and lower mountains. The **Gray-crowned Rosy-Finch** and the **Black Rosy-Finch** show up here and there across the western half of the state in winter.

*Brown-capped female*                    *Gray-crowned Rosy-Finch*

family: FINCH

*Pinicola enucleator*

**Field ID:** *Male:* Rosy-red with dark gray wings and tail; white wing bars. *Female:* Gray with a yellowish head and tail. **Size:** 9 inches.

**Habitat:** Mountain coniferous forests; piñon-juniper woodlands.

**Field Notes:** This large, plump finch with the sturdy black bill resides year-round in Colorado's coniferous forests, inhabiting higher mountains in summer, moving down into the foothills and lower elevations in winter. The Pine Grosbeak deserves its name as it is often found among the pines. Listen for its three-note call, a high-pitched whistle—*tee-wheet-tee*—going up on the central note.

*Female*

*Carpodacus cassinii*

**Field ID:** *Male:* Gray-brown upper parts heavily streaked with white; distinct streaks on sides; white belly; bright red crown; reddish throat and breast. *Female:* Heavily streaked brown and white. **Size:** 6¼ inches.

**Habitat:** High mountain coniferous forests; piñon-juniper woodlands; other areas during migration.

**Field Notes:** The Cassin's Finch is slightly larger than its more common cousin, the House Finch. The top of its head bears a complete cap of red, while the House Finch has a red brow, face, and breast. Where the Cassin's shows up in Colorado in summer, and in what numbers, depends upon the availability of food. It nests in mountain coniferous forests, moving to lower elevations for winter. In late summer the Cassin's Finch can be abundant in areas where the pine nut crop is good.

*Female*

family: FINCH

# HOUSE FINCH

*Carpodacus mexicanus*

**Field ID:** *Male:* Brownish-gray; bright red or orange brow, throat, and rump. *Female:* Gray-brown; paler, streaked undersides. **Size:** 6 inches.

**Habitat:** Urban and suburban parks and yards; riparian areas; piñon-juniper woodlands; shrublands; farm and ranch land.

**Field Notes:** The House Finch is well named, finding an abundance of food, water, and shelter around human habitation. Urban dwellers with backyard bird feeders will recognize the House Finch as one of their most common visitors. The

male's bright red plumage brings a welcome spot of color especially in winter, and in spring his cheery song, a cascade of tumbling notes, is a delight. House Finches are found throughout Colorado year-round, though more commonly at lower elevations.

*Female*

**Jan Feb Mar Apr May June July Aug Sept Oct Nov Dec**

*Loxia curvirostra*

**Field ID:** *Male:* Bright brick-red; dusky wings and tail. *Female:* Dusky with a yellowish wash; dark wings and tail. Both have a twisted bill with the tip of the upper mandible bent over and down, and the lower mandible bent up. **Size:** 6¼ inches.

**Habitat:** Coniferous forests, especially of ponderosa pine; urban and suburban coniferous landscaping.

**Field Notes:** Birds evolve all sorts of adaptive tools to help them in their particular lifestyle, and the beak of the crossbill is an extreme example. The tips of the upper and lower mandibles twist so they bend one over the other. This "crossed bill" is specialized for prying the nuts out of pine cones. Crossbills are irregular inhabitants of Colorado's coniferous forests from the mountains west. They are wayward travelers, their distribution and abundance governed by the pine nut crop. Crossbills may show up in great numbers at a site one year and be absent the next.

*Female*

family: FINCH

# PINE SISKIN

*Carduelis pinus*

**Field ID:** Streaky brown with paler underparts. In flight the yellow patches on the dark wings and the yellow on the tail are conspicuous. **Size:** 5 inches.

**Habitat:** Mountain coniferous and aspen forests; riparian areas; roadsides; shrublands; urban areas.

**Field Notes:** This little finch looks like a small brown sparrow until it takes flight, when the flash of yellow on its wings identifies it as a siskin. Its buzzy *shereee* call is also a good clue. Siskins, common in mountain forests in summer, become abundant along foothills and mountain roadsides in late summer and fall as they feed on the seeds of thistles, sunflowers, and other weeds and flowers. Siskins are found in summer from Eastern Slope foothills west across the state. In winter they may flock to foothills and lower elevation feeders.

Jan Feb **Mar Apr May** June July **Aug Sept Oct** Nov Dec

*Carduelis psaltria*

**Field ID:** *Male:* Greenish back; black head; bright yellow underparts and throat; white wing patches. *Female:* Greenish-gray with pale yellow underparts; black wings with white patches.
**Size:** 4½ inches.

**Habitat:** Riparian woodlands; shrublands; ponderosa pine forests; weedy roadsides; urban and suburban landscaping.

**Field Notes:** This handsome little finch, a summer visitor primarily in foothills areas in southern Colorado, breeds in oak-brush shrublands, riparian areas, and ponderosa pine forests. In late summer and fall, Lesser Goldfinches, which are much less common than American Goldfinches, flock to weedy roadsides and old fields to feast on thistle and other weed seeds. While male Lesser Goldfinches in other parts of the Southwest have black backs, most of Colorado's lessers are greenish-black.

*Female*

family: FINCH

*Carduelis tristis*

**Field ID:** *Breeding plumage—Male:* Bright yellow with black forehead, wings, and tail. *Female:* Olive-yellow with dark wings marked with white. *Winter plumage—Male:* Yellow-gray with yellowish face; black wings with white bars. *Female:* Grayish-brown with dark wings. **Size:** 5 inches.

**Habitat:** Riparian woodlands and adjacent fields; weedy roadsides; farm and ranch land; urban and suburban areas.

**Field Notes:** Bright describes not only the goldfinch's stunning yellow color but its cheery, twittering song and its behavior as it busily gathers seeds from roadside thistles. These noxious weeds may be a

bane to humans, but the goldfinches, often nicknamed "wild canaries," love thistle seeds. Garden flowers such as cosmos, zinnias, sunflowers, coreopsis, asters, and others, if let go to seed, will attract their interest as well. Much of the year, goldfinches are particularly found along major river drainages in all but the high mountains.

*Female*

Mary Taylor Gray's Colorado Birding Tip
**American Goldfinches**

At summer's end, with most of the flowers faded and the grass and vegetation dried to golden brown, Colorado's country roadsides seem less than attractive. But there's a jewel hiden among the weeds. The American Goldfinch feasts there on a banquet of seeds, the male's sunflower-yellow plumage and black cap making weedy roadsides a bright delight in late summer. Lesser Goldfinches and Pine Siskins are also common roadside seedeaters that may flush in flocks as you approach.

family: FINCH

**Jan Feb Mar Apr May June July Aug Sept Oct Nov Dec**

*Coccothraustes vespertinus*

**Field ID:** *Male:* Golden-yellow body; dark head with bright yellow brow; black and white wings. *Female:* Brownish-gray with yellow nape; black and white wings. Bill of both sexes is very large and heavy, colored greenish in summer, turning yellow in winter. **Size:** 8 inches.

**Habitat:** Mountain coniferous forests; suburban evergreen landscaping; riparian woodlands.

**Field Notes:** The male Evening Grosbeak perched in a pine tree is a treat to discover, his golden-yellow and black plumage in strong counterpoint to the dark green of the pine needles. Listen for his cheery warbling song. Evening Grosbeaks show up irregularly throughout the year in foothills and lower elevation mountains across the state. They are a bright and welcome winter visitor to foothills bird feeders, often flocking in to feed, then all fluttering off together.

*Female*

family: FINCH

# COLORADO BIRDING HOT SPOTS

Most of these locations are on public land and are local, county, state, or national parks or public recreation areas. Though not listed, most national forests statewide also offer good birding. Destinations on private land are not mentioned.

## Northeast
Bonny Reservoir/South Republican State Wildlife Area
Jackson Lake State Park
Pawnee National Grassland, Weld County
Tamarack Ranch State Wildlife Area

## North Central
Guanella Pass
Rocky Mountain National Park

## Denver Metro Area
Barr Lake State Park
Castlewood Canyon State Park
Chatfield State Park
Dakota Hogback Hawkwatch
Rocky Mountain Arsenal National Wildlife Refuge
South Platte River Greenway
Waterton Canyon

## Southeast
Carrizo and Cottonwood Canyons
Comanche National Grassland
John Martin Reservoir
Picketwire Canyonlands
Pueblo Reservoir
Trinidad Lake State Park Wildlife Viewing Site

## South Central
Alamosa National Wildlife Refuge
Bear Creek Canyon Regional Park
Monte Vista National Wildlife Refuge
Mueller State Park
Russell Lakes State Wildlife Area

## Southwest
Black Canyon of the Gunnison National Monument
Mesa Verde National Park

## Northwest
Arapaho National Wildlife Refuge
Colorado National Monument
Dinosaur National Monument
Hidden, Teal, and Big Creek Lakes, Mount Zirkel Wilderness Area

# COLORADO BIRDING RESOURCES

## BOOKS

*A Birder's Guide to Colorado,* Harold Holt, American Birding Association, 1997, $21.95.

*Colorado Birds, A Reference to Their Distribution and Habitat,* Robert Andrews and Robert Righter, Denver Museum of Natural History, 1992, $24.95.

*Colorado Wildlife Viewing Guide,* Mary Taylor Gray, Falcon Press, 1992, $9.95.

## ORGANIZATIONS

**Aiken Audubon Society,** P.O. Box 7616, Colorado Springs, CO 80933.

**American Birding Association,** P.O. Box 6599, Colorado Springs, CO 80934; 719-578-1614; 1-800-850-2473.

**Arkansas Valley Audubon Society,** P.O. Box 11187, Pueblo, CO 81001.

**Black Canyon Audubon Society,** P.O. Box 1371, Paonia, CO 81428.

**Boulder County Audubon Society,** P.O. Box 2081, Boulder, CO 80306.

**Colorado Bird Observatory,** 13401 Piccadilly Road, Brighton, CO 80601; 303-659-4348.

**Colorado Rare Bird Alert,** 303-424-2144.

**Denver Audubon Society,** 3000 S. Jamaica Ct., Ste. 100, Aurora, CO 80014; 303-696-0877.

**Denver Field Ornithologists,** Zoology Dept., Denver Museum of Natural History, 2001 Colorado Boulevard, Denver, CO 80205.

**Evergreen Naturalists Audubon Society,** P.O. Box 523, Evergreen, CO 80439.

**Ft. Collins Audubon Society,** P.O. Box 271968, Ft. Collins, CO 80527.

**Grand Valley Audubon Society,** P.O. Box 1211, Grand Junction, CO 81502.

**National Audubon Society,** Field Support Services Office, 3109 28th St., Boulder, CO 80301; 303-499-0219.

**Platte & Prairie Audubon Society,** P.O. Box 3413, Greeley, CO 80633.

**Roaring Fork Audubon Society,** P.O. Box 971, Glenwood, CO 81601.

**San Juan Audubon Society,** P.O. Box 2716, Durango, CO 81302.

# COLORADO SPECIES CHECKLIST IN AMERICAN ORNITHOLOGIST'S UNION (AOU) ORDER

ORDER GAVIIFORMES
**Family Gaviidae: Loons**
❏ Common Loon *Gavia immer*

ORDER PODICIPEDIFORMES
**Family Podicipedidae: Grebes**
❏ Pied-billed Grebe *Podilymbus podiceps*
❏ Horned Grebe *Podiceps auritus*
❏ Eared Grebe *Podiceps nigricollis*
❏ Western Grebe *Aechmophorus occidentalis*
❏ Clark's Grebe *Aechmophorus clarkii*

ORDER PELECANIFORMES
**Family Pelecanidae: Pelicans**
❏ American White Pelican *Pelecanus erythrorhynchos*

**Family Phalacrocoracidae: Cormorants**
❏ Double-crested Cormorant *Phalacrocorax auritus*

ORDER CICONIIFORMES
**Family Ardeidae: Bitterns and Herons**
❏ American Bittern *Botaurus lentiginosus*
❏ Great Blue Heron *Ardea herodias*
❏ Snowy Egret *Egretta thula*
❏ Cattle Egret *Bubulcus ibis*
❏ Black-crowned Night-Heron *Nycticorax nycticorax*
❏ Yellow-crowned Night-Heron *Nyctanassa violacea*

**Family Threskiornithidae: Ibises and Spoonbills**
❏ White-faced Ibis *Plegadis chihi*

**Family Cathartidae: American Vultures**
❏ Turkey Vulture *Cathartes aura*

ORDER ANSERIFORMES
**Family Anatidae: Swans, Geese, and Ducks**
❏ Tundra Swan *Cygnus columbianus*
❏ Snow Goose *Chen caerulescens*
❏ Canada Goose *Branta canadensis*
❏ Wood Duck *Aix sponsa*
❏ Green-winged Teal *Anas crecca*
❏ Mallard *Anas platyrhynchos*
❏ Northern Pintail *Anas acuta*
❏ Blue-winged Teal *Anas discors*
❏ Cinnamon Teal *Anas cyanoptera*
❏ Northern Shoveler *Anas clypeata*
❏ Gadwall *Anas strepera*
❏ American Wigeon *Anas americana*

❑ Canvasback *Aythya valisineria*
❑ Redhead *Aythya americana*
❑ Ring-necked Duck *Aythya collaris*
❑ Lesser Scaup *Aythya affinis*
❑ Common Goldeneye *Bucephala clangula*
❑ Bufflehead *Bucephala albeola*
❑ Hooded Merganser *Lophodytes cucullatus*
❑ Common Merganser *Mergus merganser*
❑ Red-breasted Merganser *Mergus serrator*
❑ Ruddy Duck *Oxyura jamaicensis*

ORDER FALCONIFORMES
**Family Accipitridae: Kites, Hawks, Eagles, and Allies**
❑ Osprey *Pandion haliaetus*
❑ Mississippi Kite *Ictinia mississippiensis*
❑ Bald Eagle *Haliaeetus leucocephalus*
❑ Northern Harrier *Circus cyaneus*
❑ Sharp-shinned Hawk *Accipiter striatus*
❑ Cooper's Hawk *Accipiter cooperii*
❑ Northern Goshawk *Accipiter gentilis*
❑ Swainson's Hawk *Buteo swainsoni*
❑ Red-tailed Hawk *Buteo jamaicensis*
❑ Ferruginous Hawk *Buteo regalis*
❑ Rough-legged Hawk *Buteo lagopus*
❑ Golden Eagle *Aquila chrysaetos*

**Family Falconidae: Caracaras and Falcons**
❑ American Kestrel *Falco sparverius*
❑ Merlin *Falco columbarius*
❑ Prairie Falcon *Falco mexicanus*
❑ Peregrine Falcon *Falco peregrinus*

ORDER GALLIFORMES
**Family Phasianidae: Partridges, Grouse, Turkeys, and Quail**
❑ Ring-necked Pheasant *Phasianus colchicus*
❑ Blue Grouse *Dendragapus obscurus*
❑ White-tailed Ptarmigan *Lagopus leucurus*
❑ Sage Grouse *Centrocercus urophasianus*
❑ Greater Prairie-Chicken *Tympanuchus cupido*
❑ Lesser Prairie-Chicken *Tympanuchus pallidicinctus*
❑ Sharp-tailed Grouse *Tympanuchus phasianellus*
❑ Wild Turkey *Meleagris gallopavo*
❑ Northern Bobwhite *Colinus virginianus*
❑ Scaled Quail *Callipepla squamata*
❑ Gambel's Quail *Callipepla gambelii*

ORDER GRUIFORMES
**Family Rallidae: Rails, Gallinules, and Coots**
❑ Virginia Rail *Rallus limicola*
❑ Sora *Porzana carolina*
❑ American Coot *Fulica americana*

**Family Gruidae: Cranes**
❑ Sandhill Crane *Grus canadensis*
❑ Whooping Crane *Grus americana*

## ORDER CHARADRIIFORMES

### Family Charadriidae: Plovers and Lapwings
- ❑ Black-bellied Plover *Pluvialis squatarola*
- ❑ Snowy Plover *Charadrius alexandrinus*
- ❑ Semipalmated Plover *Charadrius semipalmatus*
- ❑ Piping Plover *Charadrius melodus*
- ❑ Killdeer *Charadrius vociferus*
- ❑ Mountain Plover *Charadrius montanus*

### Family Recurvirostridae: Stilts and Avocets
- ❑ Black-necked Stilt *Himantopus mexicanus*
- ❑ American Avocet *Recurvirostra americana*

### Family Scolopacidae: Sandpipers, Phalaropes, and Allies
- ❑ Greater Yellowlegs *Tringa melanoleuca*
- ❑ Lesser Yellowlegs *Tringa flavipes*
- ❑ Solitary Sandpiper *Tringa solitaria*
- ❑ Willet *Catoptrophorus semipalmatus*
- ❑ Spotted Sandpiper *Actitis macularia*
- ❑ Upland Sandpiper *Bartramia longicauda*
- ❑ Long-billed Curlew *Numenius americanus*
- ❑ Marbled Godwit *Limosa fedoa*
- ❑ Semipalmated Sandpiper *Calidris pusilla*
- ❑ Western Sandpiper *Calidris mauri*
- ❑ Least Sandpiper *Calidris minutilla*
- ❑ White-rumped Sandpiper *Calidris fuscicollis*
- ❑ Baird's Sandpiper *Calidris bairdii*
- ❑ Pectoral Sandpiper *Calidris melanotos*
- ❑ Stilt Sandpiper *Calidris himantopus*
- ❑ Long-billed Dowitcher *Limnodromus scolopaceus*
- ❑ Common Snipe *Gallinago gallinago*
- ❑ Wilson's Phalarope *Phalaropus tricolor*
- ❑ Red-necked Phalarope *Phalaropus lobatus*

### Family Laridae: Skuas, Gulls, Terns, and Skimmers
- ❑ Franklin's Gull *Larus pipixcan*
- ❑ Ring-billed Gull *Larus delawarensis*
- ❑ California Gull *Larus californicus*
- ❑ Herring Gull *Larus argentatus*
- ❑ Forster's Tern *Sterna forsteri*
- ❑ Least Tern *Sterna antillarum*
- ❑ Black Tern *Chlidonias niger*

## ORDER COLUMBIFORMES

### Family Columbidae: Pigeons and Doves
- ❑ Rock Dove *Columba livia*
- ❑ Band-tailed Pigeon *Columba fasciata*
- ❑ Mourning Dove *Zenaida macroura*

## ORDER CUCULIFORMES

### Family Cuculidae: Cuckoos, Roadrunners, and Anis
- ❑ Greater Roadrunner *Geococcyx californianus*

## ORDER STRIGIFORMES
**Family Tytonidae: Barn Owls**
- ❏ Barn Owl *Tyto alba*

**Family Strigidae: Typical Owls**
- ❏ Flammulated Owl *Otus flammeolus*
- ❏ Eastern Screech-Owl *Otus asio*
- ❏ Western Screech-Owl *Otus kennicottii*
- ❏ Great Horned Owl *Bubo virginianus*
- ❏ Burrowing Owl *Athene cunicularia*
- ❏ Long-eared Owl *Asio otus*
- ❏ Short-eared Owl *Asio flammeus*
- ❏ Northern Saw-whet Owl *Aegolius acadicus*

## ORDER CAPRIMULGIFORMES
**Family Caprimulgidae: Goatsuckers**
- ❏ Common Nighthawk *Chordeiles minor*
- ❏ Common Poorwill *Phalaenoptilus nuttallii*

## ORDER APODIFORMES
**Family Apodidae: Swifts**
- ❏ Black Swift *Cypseloides niger*
- ❏ Chimney Swift *Chaetura pelagica*
- ❏ White-throated Swift *Aeronautes saxatalis*

**Family Trochilidae: Hummingbirds**
- ❏ Black-chinned Hummingbird *Archilochus alexandri*
- ❏ Calliope Hummingbird *Stellula calliope*
- ❏ Broad-tailed Hummingbird *Selasphorus platycercus*
- ❏ Rufous Hummingbird *Selasphorus rufus*

## ORDER CORACIIFORMES
**Family Alcedinidae: Kingfishers**
- ❏ Belted Kingfisher *Ceryle alcyon*

## ORDER PICIFORMES
**Family Picidae: Woodpeckers and Allies**
- ❏ Lewis's Woodpecker *Melanerpes lewis*
- ❏ Red-headed Woodpecker *Melanerpes erythrocephalus*
- ❏ Red-bellied Woodpecker *Melanerpes carolinus*
- ❏ Red-naped Sapsucker *Sphyrapicus nuchalis*
- ❏ Williamson's Sapsucker *Sphyrapicus thyroideus*
- ❏ Downy Woodpecker *Picoides pubescens*
- ❏ Hairy Woodpecker *Picoides villosus*
- ❏ Northern Flicker *Colaptes auratus*

## ORDER PASSERIFORMES
**Family Tyrannidae: Tyrant Flycatchers**
- ❏ Olive-sided Flycatcher *Contopus cooperi*
- ❏ Western Wood-Pewee *Contopus sordidulus*
- ❏ Willow Flycatcher *Empidonax traillii*
- ❏ Hammond's Flycatcher *Empidonax hammondii*
- ❏ Dusky Flycatcher *Empidonax oberholseri*

❑ Gray Flycatcher *Empidonax wrightii*
❑ Cordilleran Flycatcher *Empidonax occidentalis*
❑ Say's Phoebe *Sayornis saya*
❑ Ash-throated Flycatcher *Myiarchus cinerascens*
❑ Cassin's Kingbird *Tyrannus vociferans*
❑ Western Kingbird *Tyrannus verticalis*
❑ Eastern Kingbird *Tyrannus tyrannus*

**Family Alaudidae: Larks**
❑ Horned Lark *Eremophila alpestris*

**Family Hirundinidae: Swallows**
❑ Purple Martin *Progne subis*
❑ Tree Swallow *Tachycineta bicolor*
❑ Violet-green Swallow *Tachycineta thalassina*
❑ Northern Rough-winged Swallow *Stelgidopteryx serripennis*
❑ Bank Swallow *Riparia riparia*
❑ Cliff Swallow *Petrochelidon pyrrhonota*
❑ Barn Swallow *Hirundo rustica*

**Family Corvidae: Jays, Magpies, and Crows**
❑ Gray Jay *Perisoreus canadensis*
❑ Steller's Jay *Cyanocitta stelleri*
❑ Blue Jay *Cyanocitta cristata*
❑ Western Scrub-Jay *Aphelocoma californica*
❑ Pinyon Jay *Gymnorhinus cyanocephalus*
❑ Clark's Nutcracker *Nucifraga columbiana*
❑ Black-billed Magpie *Pica pica*
❑ American Crow *Corvus brachyrhynchos*
❑ Common Raven *Corvus corax*

**Family Paridae: Titmice**
❑ Black-capped Chickadee *Poecile atricapillus*
❑ Mountain Chickadee *Poecile gambeli*
❑ Juniper Titmouse *Baeolophus ridgwayi*

**Family Aegithalidae: Bushtits**
❑ Bushtit *Psaltriparus minimus*

**Family Sittidae: Nuthatches**
❑ Red-breasted Nuthatch *Sitta canadensis*
❑ White-breasted Nuthatch *Sitta carolinensis*
❑ Pygmy Nuthatch *Sitta pygmaea*

**Family Certhiidae: Creepers**
❑ Brown Creeper *Certhia americana*

**Family Troglodytidae: Wrens**
❑ Rock Wren *Salpinctes obsoletus*
❑ Canyon Wren *Catherpes mexicanus*
❑ Bewick's Wren *Thryomanes bewickii*
❑ House Wren *Troglodytes aedon*
❑ Marsh Wren *Cistothorus palustris*

**Family Cinclidae: Dippers**
❑ American Dipper *Cinclus mexicanus*

**Family Regulidae: Kinglets**
❑ Golden-crowned Kinglet *Regulus satrapa*
❑ Ruby-crowned Kinglet *Regulus calendula*

**Family Muscicapidae: Old World Warblers, Gnatcatchers, Old World Flycatchers, Thrushes, and Wrentit**
❑ Blue-gray Gnatcatcher *Polioptila caerulea*
❑ Eastern Bluebird *Sialia sialis*
❑ Western Bluebird *Sialia mexicana*
❑ Mountain Bluebird *Sialia currucoides*
❑ Townsend's Solitaire *Myadestes townsendi*
❑ Swainson's Thrush *Catharus ustulatus*
❑ Hermit Thrush *Catharus guttatus*
❑ American Robin *Turdus migratorius*

**Family Mimidae: Mockingbirds, Thrashers, and Allies**
❑ Gray Catbird *Dumetella carolinensis*
❑ Northern Mockingbird *Mimus polyglottos*
❑ Sage Thrasher *Oreoscoptes montanus*
❑ Brown Thrasher *Toxostoma rufum*

**Family Motacillidae: Wagtails and Pipits**
❑ American Pipit *Anthus rubescens*

**Family Bombycillidae: Waxwings**
❑ Bohemian Waxwing *Bombycilla garrulus*
❑ Cedar Waxwing *Bombycilla cedrorum*

**Family Laniidae: Shrikes**
❑ Northern Shrike *Lanius excubitor*
❑ Loggerhead Shrike *Lanius ludovicianus*

**Family Sturnidae: Starlings and Allies**
❑ European Starling *Sturnus vulgaris*

**Family Vireonidae: Vireos**
❑ Bell's Vireo *Vireo bellii*
❑ Plumbeous Vireo *Vireo plumbeus*
❑ Warbling Vireo *Vireo gilvus*

**Family Parulideae: Wood-Warblers**
❑ Orange-crowned Warbler *Vermivora celata*
❑ Virginia's Warbler *Vermivora virginiae*
❑ Yellow Warbler *Dendroica petechia*
❑ Yellow-rumped Warbler *Dendroica coronata*
❑ Black-throated Gray Warbler *Dendroica nigrescens*
❑ Townsend's Warbler *Dendroica townsendi*
❑ MacGillivray's Warbler *Oporornis tolmiei*
❑ Common Yellowthroat *Geothlypis trichas*
❑ Wilson's Warbler *Wilsonia pusilla*
❑ Yellow-breasted Chat *Icteria virens*

**Family Thraupidae: Tanagers**
❑ Western Tanager *Piranga ludoviciana*

**Family Cardinalidae: Cardinals, Grosbeaks, and Buntings**
❏ Black-headed Grosbeak *Pheucticus melanocephalus*
❏ Blue Grosbeak *Guiraca caerulea*
❏ Lazuli Bunting *Passerina amoena*

**Family Emberizidae: Sparrows, Blackbirds, and Allies**
❏ Green-tailed Towhee *Pipilo chlorurus*
❏ Spotted Towhee *Pipilo maculatus*
❏ Canyon Towhee *Pipilo fuscus*
❏ Cassin's Sparrow *Aimophila cassinii*
❏ American Tree Sparrow *Spizella arborea*
❏ Chipping Sparrow *Spizella passerina*
❏ Clay-colored Sparrow *Spizella pallida*
❏ Brewer's Sparrow *Spizella breweri*
❏ Vesper Sparrow *Pooecetes gramineus*
❏ Lark Sparrow *Chondestes grammacus*
❏ Sage Sparrow *Amphispiza belli*
❏ Lark Bunting *Calamospiza melanocorys*
❏ Savannah Sparrow *Passerculus sandwichensis*
❏ Grasshopper Sparrow *Ammodramus savannarum*
❏ Song Sparrow *Melospiza melodia*
❏ Lincoln's Sparrow *Melospiza lincolnii*
❏ White-crowned Sparrow *Zonotrichia leucophrys*
❏ Harris's Sparrow *Zonotrichia querula*
❏ Dark-eyed Junco *Junco hyemalis*
❏ McCown's Longspur *Calcarius mccownii*
❏ Lapland Longspur *Calcarius lapponicus*
❏ Chestnut-collared Longspur *Calcarius ornatus*
❏ Bobolink *Dolichonyx oryzivorus*
❏ Red-winged Blackbird *Agelaius phoeniceus*
❏ Western Meadowlark *Sturnella neglecta*
❏ Yellow-headed Blackbird *Xanthocephalus xanthocephalus*
❏ Brewer's Blackbird *Euphagus cyanocephalus*
❏ Great-tailed Grackle *Quiscalus mexicanus*
❏ Common Grackle *Quiscalus quiscula*
❏ Brown-headed Cowbird *Molothrus ater*
❏ Orchard Oriole *Icterus spurius*
❏ Bullock's Oriole *Icterus bullockii*

**Family Fringillidae: Fringilline and
Cardueline Finches and Allies**
❏ Gray-crowned Rosy-Finch *Leucosticte tephrocotis*
❏ Black Rosy-Finch *Leucosticte atratus*
❏ Brown-capped Rosy-Finch *Leucosticte australis*
❏ Pine Grosbeak *Pinicola enucleator*
❏ Cassin's Finch *Carpodacus cassinii*
❏ House Finch *Carpodacus mexicanus*
❏ Red Crossbill *Loxia curvirostra*
❏ Pine Siskin *Carduelis pinus*
❏ Lesser Goldfinch *Carduelis psaltria*
❏ American Goldfinch *Carduelis tristis*
❏ Evening Grosbeak *Coccothraustes vespertinus*

**Family Passeridae: Old World Sparrows**
❏ House Sparrow *Passer domesticus*

# INDEX

# Index

# ABOUT THE AUTHOR
## Mary Taylor Gray

Noted Colorado bird and wildlife writer Mary Taylor Gray spent her childhood summers roaming the Colorado Rockies from her grandparents' cabin in Estes Park. "We awoke to mule deer peering in the windows and hummingbirds buzzing the red-trimmed feeders," she recalls. Her love of Colorado's outdoor and wildlife heritage led to a degree in zoology from Colorado State University and a life devoted to birds and nature.

A professional nature writer specializing in birdwatching and wildlife viewing, she is the author of six books, including *Watchable Birds of the Rocky Mountains* and *Colorado Wildlife Viewing Guide*. Many Coloradans know Mary from her *Words on Birds* column appearing monthly in the *Rocky Mountain News*, while other nature-lovers are familiar with her lively style from *Colorado's Wildlife Company*, a quarterly publication she writes for the Colorado Division of Wildlife's Watchable Wildlife program. Mary has written hundreds of magazine and newspaper articles for such publications as *Colorado Outdoors, Birder's World, Birdwatcher's Digest,* and *Outside*. She also writes extensively for the Rocky Mountain Arsenal National Wildlife Refuge.

Mary sits on the Board of Directors of the Denver Audubon Society, is a member of the Colorado Authors League and Outdoor Writers Association of America, and teaches summer nature writing workshops at Rocky Mountain National Park.

Mary writes and watches birds from her home in Denver, where she lives with her husband, Richard Young, and daughter, Olivia.

# ABOUT THE PHOTOGRAPHER
## Herbert Clarke

An avid birder since childhood, Herbert Clarke has studied and photographed birds all over the world with special emphasis on western North America. He is the author of several popular books, and his articles and photographs have appeared in many books, magazines, and natural history publications. Each year, in addition to his frequent travels, he leads tours, gives illustrated lectures, and instructs classes on birds. Herbert lives in Glendale, California, with his wife and constant field companion, Olga.

**Color Tab Index to Bird Categories**